Sampling
and the Census

Sampling and the Census

A Case against the Proposed Adjustments for Undercount

Kenneth Darga

The AEI Press

Publisher for the American Enterprise Institute
WASHINGTON, D.C.

1999

Available in the United States from the AEI Press, c/o Publisher Resources Inc., 1224 Heil Quaker Blvd., P.O. Box 7001, La Vergne, TN 37086-7001. Distributed outside the United States by arrangement with Eurospan, 3 Henrietta Street, London WC2E 8LU England.

Library of Congress Cataloging-in-Publication Data

Darga, Kenneth.
    Sampling and the census : a case against the proposed adjustments for undercount / Kenneth Darga.
       p. cm.
    ISBN 0-8447-4102-7 (paper : alk. paper)
    1. United States—Census—Methodology. 2. United States—Census, 22nd, 2000—Methodology. 3. Sampling (Statistics)
    4. Census undercounts—United States. I. Title.
HA179.D37   1999
304.6'0723—dc21   99-11413
                                         CIP

THE AEI PRESS
Publisher for the American Enterprise Institute
1150 17th Street, N.W., Washington, D.C. 20036

Printed in the United States of America

Contents

Figures

Foreword

As we all know, the decennial census mandated by the Constitution is a matter of great importance. The census provides the basis for establishing political boundaries, including boundaries for state and local political districts as well as congressional districts. It also serves as a basis for fund allocation: not only federal funds, but state, local, and private funds are often distributed on the basis of census data. The census enables scholars, government officials, business people, planners, and citizens to understand trends and developments in individual communities as well as in the nation as a whole.

The census is not, and never has been, 100 percent accurate. It misses some people, though the two most recent censuses have apparently missed less than 2 percent of the total. The great issue facing us as the census for the year 2000 approaches is this: Will the effort to make the census more accurate by adjusting for undercount cause it instead to be less accurate?

The adjustment process involves the use of sampling, and the casual newspaper reader might get the impression that the debate is over the validity of sampling and its legality in conducting the census. The political and legal battle has taken that form. But the real scientific debate is not over sampling as a technique. Sampling is a well-established statistical tool with many very useful functions. This volume makes it clear that the critical debate is over the proposed adjustment method itself, not the use of sampling as such. As the author points out, even an otherwise valid statistical analysis tends to produce faulty results when it relies on faulty data and faulty assumptions. He is persuaded on the basis of extensive analysis that the proposed adjustment of the census would introduce a whole new set of errors in seeking to cure the undercount. The issues are not simple, but the risks of making a wrong decision are great.

We at AEI believe it is important that the debate be brought back into focus. Dealing with undercount in the census is an exceptionally difficult problem at best. The Census Bureau may be off on a very misguided track.

CHRISTOPHER DEMUTH
President, American Enterprise Institute

Preface

The development of this volume has spanned much of the past decade, and it reflects assistance and encouragement that I have received from many different people.

Many of the arguments in this volume were originally developed for an analysis that I submitted to the Census Bureau in 1992. That analysis was a response to the bureau's request for professional review of its proposal to use adjusted census counts as a basis for population estimates, and it contributed to the eventual decision not to use the adjustments for that purpose. I refined and expanded those arguments in 1997, after it came to my attention that the new adjustment methodology had the same shortcomings that had been identified at the beginning of the decade. I sent several preliminary versions of chapters 2 and 3 to the Census Bureau, beginning in the summer of 1997.

Those papers eventually came to the attention of the House Subcommittee on the Census, and I was called on to present them to the subcommittee in testimony on May 5, 1998. Following that testimony, I was asked to answer a series of questions from the ranking minority member of the subcommittee, and the Census Bureau was asked to develop an official response addressing all my criticisms of its proposed methodology. My answers to the questions are contained in Appendix A of this volume, and the Census Bureau's response to chapters 2 and 3 is contained in Appendix B, along with my rejoinder.

Current and former personnel of the Census Bureau have provided valuable assistance by answering my questions, providing information, and helping to confirm many of my findings and identify ambiguities and errors in the early drafts of these materials. Several statisticians and demographers outside the bureau have also provided valuable assistance, as well as assurance that I am not alone in my skepticism regarding the proposed methodology. David Freedman (University of California, Berkeley) has provided many helpful suggestions, as have his colleagues Philip Stark and Kenneth Wachter. Jerry Coffey (formerly of the U.S. Office of Management and Budget) has also provided valuable assistance. I am especially indebted to Leo Breiman (University of California, Berkeley), whose analysis of the Census Bureau's evaluation reports on the 1990 adjustment process provided much of the basis for chapter 3.

I am also grateful to the members and staff of the Subcommittee on the Census for their responses to my testimony, and to Marvin Kosters and others at the American Enterprise Institute who proposed drawing these materials together into a book and brought that project to completion.

The debate over census undercount adjustment is likely to continue long after the current volume is published. Readers who are interested in reviewing other testimony on the adjustments and new developments in the debate may be interested in the Internet website:

http://www.stat.berkeley.edu/users/stark/census

1
Introduction

Marvin H. Kosters

The decennial census scheduled for the year 2000 carries out a requirement in the U.S. Constitution first implemented in 1790. After 200 years of experience it might seem surprising that plans for carrying out the next census—plans that have been developed by the Bureau of the Census throughout the past decade and shaped by research, deliberations, and reports by the prestigious National Research Council—should now be controversial. Nevertheless, how Census 2000 should be carried out is a highly contentious issue involving all three branches of the federal government. The delay in selecting and planning for a specific approach threatens to reduce the efficacy of whatever procedures are eventually adopted.

The most controversial of the procedures proposed for the next census involves adjusting data from enumeration results to include estimates of the number of people who were missed. Media reports generally refer to these adjustments for undercount in terms of "census sampling," since they would be based on the results of a sample survey. Political and legal aspects of the controversy often receive most of the attention, and media reports often suggest there is a consensus among social scientists that the proposed procedure would increase the accuracy of the census. This publication, however, demonstrates that there are serious scientific arguments against the proposed procedure as well.

1

This volume is written for policymakers as well as for demographers and statisticians, and its arguments are presented in a clear and understandable manner. Nevertheless, some introduction to the underlying issues may be helpful. After addressing several background issues, these introductory comments conclude with a brief overview of the scope and contents of the volume.

Issues Underlying the Debate on "Census Sampling"

An intense controversy has arisen regarding the appropriate methods for conducting a census. Following is a consideration of the basic questions and premises underlying the census debates.

Why the Census Is Controversial. One explanation for the intense controversy about how to conduct the census is that its results have definite political and financial implications. Census data are used to determine how congressional seats are divided up among and within states, and even presidential elections are affected through the electoral college. The allocation of money and of public facilities like roads and schools is influenced by census data. Economists anticipate that adjustment for differential undercount would translate more or less directly into transfer of more budget resources to geographic areas with larger proportions of minorities and people living in rental units. Observers also widely believe that the political influence of people in areas with these characteristics would be increased through the process of drawing new boundaries for political districts. This process would thus favor liberal political candidates for public office, giving Democrats an advantage over Republicans.

These financial and political implications certainly provide ample explanation for the controversy over census procedures, but the controversy has another important basis as well. Proponents of the Census Bureau's proposals believe that they would succeed in their intended purpose of making the census more accurate, and that the census would become even more suitable for the myriad important purposes for which it is used. Conversely, opponents of the proposals, including the author of this volume, argue that the census would be made much less accurate and less suitable for those purposes.

How a Conventional Census Is Conducted. Before considering the innovations proposed to correct the shortcomings of the census, it is important to understand some important aspects of how a census is conducted. The decennial census has historically been intended as a complete head count, covering everyone, and it involves several special efforts to promote a high level of accuracy. The Census Bureau works with local units of government to ensure that the address lists developed by its field staff are as complete as possible. To minimize language barriers, instructions are made available in a variety of languages—in 1990, for example, in thirty-four languages. In an effort to ensure that everyone is included, enumerators personally visit every known housing unit that has not returned a census form by mail, and they make repeated attempts to interview people who do not respond. When information cannot be obtained from a household member, enumerators use information from neighbors or others. When enumerators obtain incomplete information or no information at all about an occupied housing unit, an imputation methodology is used to supply the missing information.

Enumerators also visit shelters, places where homeless people are known to congregate, and other places where people might be found who would not otherwise be included in census figures. Publicity campaigns are conducted so that even people who are missed by other efforts can obtain a census form or be interviewed. To avoid counting people more than once, considerable effort is made to identify each person and avoid duplication. Thus, the conventional census is far more than the crude head count that it is sometimes portrayed to be.

Why It Is Difficult to Count Everyone Correctly. Despite all the efforts made to obtain an accurate count, it has long been recognized that instances occur in which the same people are counted more than once (overcount), or people who should be counted are not (undercount). Comparisons with administrative data on births, deaths, immigration, and so forth suggest that the net effect of these errors for broad aggregates is an undercount, with the extent of the undercount being greater in some segments of the population and some localities than in others.

Can counting the number of people who live in the United States really be so difficult that errors occur decade after decade? The answer, unfortunately, is "yes." It is not easy to get an accurate census count—or, for that matter, to do an accurate sample survey to measure undercount—in a large country where people move frequently, where many have more than one place of residence or are not at home, where living arrangements are varied and not always consistent with local codes or lease arrangements, and where many people have personal reasons to avoid enumeration. It is inevitable that any census—as well as any undercount survey—will miss some of the people who should be counted.

Proposed New Uses of Sampling. Two new uses of sampling outlined in the Census 2000 plans have proved to be highly controversial. One would adjust the count for the population as a whole and for each component—as defined by age, race, sex, home ownership status, type of community, and state of residence—for its apparent overcount or undercount in the census. These adjustments would be based on a sample survey conducted after the census, which would be matched with census responses to determine who was missed by the census and who was counted in error. The accuracy of such adjustments is the primary focus of this volume.

The second proposal involves reliance on sampling for following up on non-response to census questionnaires in each census subdivision or tract. Such sampling would replace the laborious, costly, and not fully accurate method of trying to follow up on all non-respondents. It is intended mainly to save money without sacrificing accuracy, and it is hoped that perhaps sampling may even improve accuracy if a substantially higher response rate can be elicited in the sample than would otherwise be obtained. This volume discusses sampling for non-response only briefly in Appendix A.

Why New Procedures Are Being Explored. In its description of the Census 2000 plan, the Census Bureau claims that "the census in 1990 took a step backward on the fundamental issue of accuracy. For the first time since the Census Bureau began conducting post-census evaluations in 1940, the decennial census was less accurate than its predecessor."[1] Although the censuses of 1980 and 1990 were the most accurate in history, this interpretation of the 1990 data as showing a deterioration in accuracy lent support to a conclusion that "there was a consensus among the Census Bureau, professional statisticians, and Congress that significant changes were required for the upcoming 2000 census; the Census Bureau could not continue to employ the methods it had been using."[2]

The resulting plan for Census 2000 is intended to improve the accuracy of the census while incurring lower

---

1. U.S. Department of Commerce, Bureau of the Census, *Report to Congress—The Plan for Census 2000,* revised and reissued, August 1997, p. 2.

2. Ibid., Executive Summary, p. ix.

costs to gather the data. A brief discussion of the size of the cost saving and its sources is useful. The cost of carrying out the Census Bureau's plan for Census 2000 is estimated at about $4 billion. The cost of conducting the census using procedures similar to those used in 1990 is estimated as being about three-quarters of a billion dollars more.[3] The estimated cost saving is mainly attributable to the substitution of sampling for non-response for more intensive efforts to enumerate everyone in every census subdivision. The costs saved by sampling for non-response would be even larger if they were not partly offset by the $200 million cost of a large post-enumeration survey sample intended for use in adjusting for undercount under the Census Bureau's plan. The estimated cost savings are significant, but they should be kept in perspective.

An Appropriate Focus for the Debate. So much of the motivation for the controversy over the census involves issues of money and power that little attention has been focused on objective scientific issues. Unfortunately, the public discussion has shown a tendency toward oversimplification. The general question of whether sampling is appropriate for use in the census is often misleadingly presented as the main issue. Purportedly, most experts defend the legitimacy of sampling, and its potential value for the census has been recognized by influential groups like the American Statistical Association and the National Academy of Sciences. The imperfections of the census are often emphasized, and proponents of complete enumeration are regarded as unscientific and politically motivated. The impasse on how to proceed is thus characterized as a problem of politics getting in the way of good science.

From a scientific standpoint, the potential value of sampling is not a very fruitful focus for debate. On the one hand, the scientific validity and legitimacy of statisti-

---

3. Ibid., pp. 37–39.

cal sampling for data collection and analysis are widely accepted. It would be difficult to rule out the possibility of someday developing methodologies involving sampling that would improve the accuracy of the census. On the other hand, even the most ardent supporter of using sampling in the census would find it difficult to deny that some methodologies might result in a decrease in accuracy. Recognition of the *potential* value of sampling—no matter how great that potential might be—is not an adequate basis for adopting the *particular* approach that has been proposed by the Census Bureau, if that approach would detract from accuracy.

Thus, a fruitful focus for the scientific debate is whether the particular approach and methodology that have been proposed would make the census better or worse.

Approach and Scope of This Volume

This study by Kenneth Darga therefore addresses the straightforward issue of whether the Census Bureau's proposed procedures to adjust for undercount can be expected to improve the accuracy of census figures, or whether instead these procedures are likely to introduce so much new error that the resulting figures are less accurate. The case for adjustment of the 1990 census for undercount was considered in the early 1990s, using data that were collected in the 1990 post-enumeration sample survey. Although a decision was made not to adjust the census and this decision was sustained in the courts, the data that were developed in 1990 have been analyzed extensively. The use of data from the Post-Enumeration Survey to adjust the enumeration for 1990 corresponds to the controversial use of such data to adjust for undercount in the Census 2000 plans.

Some details of the methodology have changed, but the concepts underlying the Census 2000 plans are similar

7

in most important respects to the approach that was followed in 1990. Unless the problems identified in the analysis of the 1990 data can be dealt with in satisfactory ways, data developed under the current plans for Census 2000 would be subject to problems of the same kind as were identified when adjustment of the 1990 census figures was rejected. Consequently, these 1990 data are a rich source for analytical insights into the effects on accuracy of using this approach to obtain information to adjust for undercount.

Some important issues are not addressed in this study. With regard to *legality*, for example, a panel of federal judges ruled that the use of sampling to develop data for use in apportionment is not consistent with federal law. This decision was appealed to the Supreme Court, and the Court has ruled on the requirements of federal law but not on the constitutionality of using sampling and adjustment procedures for the census figures that would be used for apportionment and redistricting. These legal and constitutional issues are important, but they are not considered in this analysis.

It is usually presumed that adjustment for differential undercount would result in increased budget transfers and spending for areas in which minorities, renters, and immigrants are concentrated. It is also widely believed that adjustment for differential undercount would result in changes in apportionment that would be disadvantageous for Republicans as compared with Democrats. These suppositions may well be at least partially correct, but their validity is not assessed in this analysis. A presupposition that underlies the analysis in this volume is that the accuracy and utility of the census is what counts, and the political fallout is not addressed. The focus is on implications for substantive accuracy of data that would be generated under current plans for Census 2000, based on extensive analysis of analogous data that were gathered for the 1990 census.

Overview of This Volume

The central arguments against the proposed method of adjusting for undercount are contained in chapter 2, "Straining Out Gnats and Swallowing Camels: Unintended Effects of Adjusting for Census Undercount." This chapter shows that significant errors are inevitably entailed in the proposed approach. The proposed survey to measure undercount is not capable of counting many of the people who are missed by the census; it is very sensitive even to extremely small sources of error; and it is subject to many sources of error that are very serious. Thus, many of the people who fail to participate in the census will be missed again by the survey, and other people will be falsely identified as "missed" by the census because their census response cannot be found and identified. These inevitable problems help to explain the implausible and erroneous measurements of undercount that the author found in his analysis of the 1990 survey. This chapter shows that faulty adjustments for undercount would have a disturbing effect on the accuracy and reliability of census data.

To obtain insight into the amount of error produced at subnational levels by sample-based adjustment for undercount, Darga develops an ingenious analysis that makes use of the ratio of females to males among children. He uses adjustment factors based on the Post-Enumeration Sample survey and compares these adjusted data with the actual results of the census head count enumeration. When he makes this comparison he finds that sex ratios deviate widely from the norm in the adjusted data— far more widely than in the original, unadjusted head count data. The adjusted data often show far more boys than girls in a given location, for example, although common sense suggests that this cannot be the case, and the head count data in fact show it not to be the case. Yet under the Census Bureau's plan, adjusted figures—and only adjusted figures—would be the official figures.

Darga's evidence suggests that adjustments to compensate for undercount at subnational levels can introduce new errors far more serious than the deficiencies of the data that the adjustments were intended to correct. His conclusion is that "the census is not really broken until it is fixed."

Darga uses the clearly spurious boy-girl ratios produced by the 1990 adjustment process to illustrate the potential effect of adjustment on other census results, assuming the same size and pattern of error. The findings are striking. Comparisons over time could show migration of large numbers of people from different demographic groups between major cities and geographic areas—even though no such movement occurred. The spurious changes would be entirely the result of the use of adjustment factors that are heavily contaminated by errors that are inherent in the sampling and adjustment method used. The conclusion is that the effort to adjust for undercount threatens to destroy the reliability of census data at the state and local levels.

Chapter 3, "Quantifying Measurement Error and Bias in the 1990 Undercount Estimates," uses the results of the Census Bureau's evaluation studies to show that the errors described in the preceding chapter actually occurred on a large scale in 1990.

The first appendix in this volume contains answers to twenty-five questions that were asked by Representative Carolyn Maloney, the ranking minority member of the Subcommittee on the Census, following submission of two papers (chapters 2 and 3 in this volume) to the subcommittee. These questions cover a wide range of important concerns and beliefs that are undoubtedly shared by many readers. Although the questions were apparently designed to expose any weaknesses in the arguments against the planned adjustments, the answers broaden and strengthen the case against the Census Bureau's proposal.

The second appendix contains the Census Bureau's

official response to the studies, along with the author's rejoinder. The bureau's response was prepared at the request of minority members of the subcommittee, and it raises several important issues. The rejoinder systematically lays out the bureau's response alongside the arguments that were advanced in the original studies, allowing the reader to assess the status of the debate. Of particular interest is the final section of the rejoinder, in which the author addresses three general counterarguments that were advanced by the bureau. This section shows that the proposed adjustment method is based on faulty assumptions as well as faulty data, and it sheds a great deal of light on one of the most puzzling questions in the debate over adjusting the census for undercount. Why do the adjustments that resulted in 1990 appear successful to so many analysts, when in fact they were not? The author shows that the divergence of views about the success of the adjustments is caused by a failure to resolve critical paradoxes, and that the key to resolving those paradoxes is provided by the arguments in this volume.

The use of sampling to reduce costs and improve the accuracy of the decennial census for the year 2000 has, on its face, received broad support from statisticians and social scientists. Indeed, professionals are virtually unanimous in their support of statistical sampling techniques as being useful. Contrary to the impression left by many news reports, however, the statistics profession is not unanimous in its support of the Census Bureau's specific plan for undercount adjustment. Some highly respected and experienced professionals who have analyzed the Census Bureau's plan have expressed reservations about it, and the analysis in this volume provides a very readable but powerful discussion of some of the issues and evidence that form the basis for their concerns.

11

2
Straining Out Gnats and Swallowing Camels— Unintended Effects of Adjusting for Undercount

Although the Department of Commerce is often criticized for census undercount, it is not surprising that every census misses a portion of the population. In fact, what is noteworthy is not that the undercount persists, but rather that the net undercount appears to have been less than 5 million people in 1990, or only about 1.8 percent of the population.[1]

A major reason for the undercount—although not by any means the only reason—is that quite a few people do not want their identities known by the government. For example, the United States has more than 1 million people who do not make any of their required payments on court-ordered child support,[2] as well as an estimated 5 million illegal immigrants.[3] Each year the police make more

---

1. U.S. Department of Commerce, "Census Bureau Releases Refined 1990 Census Coverage Estimates from Demographic Analysis," Press Release of June 13, 1991, table 1.

2. Economics and Statistics Administration, U.S. Department of Commerce, "Statistical Brief: Who Receives Child Support?" May 1995.

3. U.S. Immigration and Naturalization Service, "INS Releases Updated Estimates of U.S. Illegal Immigration," Press Release of February 2, 1997.

than 14 million arrests for non-traffic offenses.[4] Millions of additional criminals remain at-large; many people would lose government benefits if the actual composition of their households were known; and many people have other reasons for concealing their identity and whereabouts from the government. If the census misses fewer than 5 million people under these circumstances, then the Census Bureau is doing a truly remarkable job.

Nevertheless, eliminating even this small error would be a valuable achievement. Although the effect on many components of the population would be small, people in some demographic and economic categories are undercounted more than others. This tendency leads to anomalies and imprecision in some analyses and affects political apportionment and fund distribution. The Census Bureau has therefore tried very hard to devise ways to measure and compensate for the problem of undercount.

Obviously, these methods are intended to make the census count better. We need to evaluate their actual effects, however, instead of their intended effects. Before we decide to use these particular methods in the official population count for the year 2000, we have to determine whether they would make that population count better or worse.

After reviewing some of the reasons for believing that censuses miss a portion of the population, this chapter briefly describes the Census Bureau's proposed method of adjusting for undercount. It will then be shown that, although the results of this method for 1990 appeared plausible, at least at the broadest national aggregation, the method cannot produce reliable adjustments for undercount: it is not capable of counting many of the people who are missed by the census; it is very sensitive even to extremely small sources of error; and it is subject to many

---

4. U.S. Department of Justice, Bureau of Justice Statistics, *Sourcebook of Criminal Justice Statistics*, 1995, p. 394.

sources of error that are very serious. Thus it is not surprising to find that many of the detailed undercount measurements for 1990 were implausible and, in some cases, demonstrably false. In an effort to correct a net national undercount of less than 2 percent, spurious undercounts of 10 percent, 20 percent, and even 30 percent were identified for some segments of the population. Adjustments derived from these measurements would have had a devastating effect on the usefulness and accuracy of census data at the state and local level, and they would have had an adverse effect on nearly all purposes for which census data are used. Similar problems can be expected with the undercount adjustment proposed for Census 2000: the problems are not attributable to minor flaws in methodology or implementation, but rather to the impossibility of measuring undercount through the sort of coverage survey that has been proposed.

Evidence of Undercount in the Census

Before examining the Census Bureau's method of adjusting for undercount, it is instructive to consider how we can know that each census misses part of the population.

One way to find evidence of undercount is to project the population for a census year by applying mortality rates and migration rates to the results of other censuses. The pattern of differences between these projections and the actual census counts can provide good evidence for undercount. For example, if the count of black males aged twenty to twenty-four is lower than would be expected based on the number of black males aged ten to fourteen in the previous census, and if it is lower than would be expected based on the number of black males aged thirty to thirty-four in the following census, then there is good evidence of undercount for that segment of the population.

The most widely accepted method for measuring census undercount is called "demographic analysis." Using a combination of birth registration data, estimates of under-registration, mortality rates, estimates of international migration, social security enrollment data, and analyses of previous censuses, the Census Bureau develops estimates of the national population for each census year by age, race, and sex. Although they are not perfect, the gap between these estimates and the national census count provides the best available measure of undercount. The pattern of undercount suggested by demographic analysis is generally consistent from one census to another, and it is consistent with the discrepancies that are found between population projections and census counts. Undercount rates appear to be higher for males than for females, higher for blacks than for whites, and higher for young adults than for people in other age groups.[5]

Demographic analysis suggests that the net national undercount fell in each successive census from 5.4 percent of the population in 1940 to only 1.2 percent in 1980. This reflects improvements in census-taking methodologies, special efforts focused on segments of the population that are hard to count, and assurances that census information will be kept strictly confidential. Nevertheless, the estimated net undercount rose to 1.8 percent in the 1990 census: still quite low by historic standards, but disappointing because it represents an increase relative to the previous census (see figure 2–1 and table 2–1).

A major shortcoming of this method is that it works only at the national level: there is too much interstate and intrastate migration to allow a phenomenon as subtle as census undercount to be visible at the state or local level through demographic analysis. Since we can expect undercount to vary considerably from state to state and

---

5. J. Gregory Robinson et al., "Estimation of Population Coverage in the 1990 United States Census Based on Demographic Analysis," *Journal of the American Statistical Association*, 88(423): 1061–79.

FIGURE 2–1
UNDERCOUNT RATE FOR TOTAL POPULATION, 1940–1990

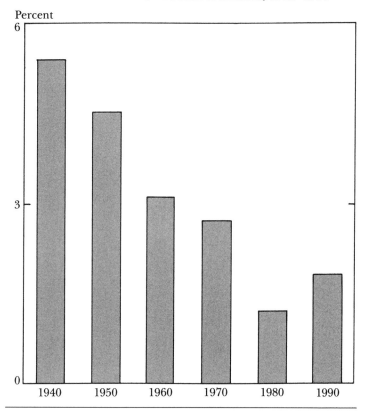

TABLE 2–1
ESTIMATES OF CENSUS UNDERCOUNT BASED ON DEMOGRAPHIC ANALYSIS, 1940–1990
(percent)

Population Category	1940	1950	1960	1970	1980	1990
Total Population	5.4	4.1	3.1	2.7	1.2	1.8
Black	8.4	7.5	6.6	6.5	4.5	5.7
Non-black	5.0	3.8	2.7	2.2	0.8	1.3

SOURCE: J. Gregory Robinson et al., "Estimation of Population Coverage in the 1990 United States Census Based on Demographic Analysis," *Journal of the American Statistical Association,* 88(423): 1061–79.

neighborhood to neighborhood, we cannot simply apply the national undercount rates to state and local population counts. This would not adjust some areas enough, and it would introduce inaccuracies into areas where there had not been inaccuracies before.

Calculating Adjustments for Undercount

The Census Bureau has therefore tried to develop additional methods to estimate how well the census covers each segment of the population. Immediately after the census count is completed, the bureau conducts a "coverage survey" that essentially repeats the population count for a small sample of census blocks. The coverage survey was called the Post-Enumeration Survey, or PES, in 1990, and it will be called the Integrated Coverage Measurement Survey, or ICM, in 2000. Data from the coverage survey are matched person-by-person with the original census to identify the individuals counted by the coverage survey who seem to have been missed by the census. These results are tabulated by relevant population characteristics to produce estimated undercount rates that can be applied to local areas based on their counts of persons with those characteristics. A sample of original census forms are also matched with the coverage survey to identify individuals who were counted by the census but omitted by the survey. These discrepancies are investigated and used to estimate "erroneous enumerations" or overcount.

Apparent Plausibility of the Adjustments

The resulting adjustment to the 1990 Census seemed quite plausible at the broadest national level. After moving up and down as corrections were made to the data and new statistical techniques were applied, the estimate of overall net undercount at the national level was 1.6 per-

17

cent[6]—very close to the 1.8 percent suggested by demographic analysis. The credibility of the 1990 coverage survey was increased by the fact that it suggested high rates of undercount at the national level for the groups that would be expected to have high undercounts, such as Hispanics, blacks, people with difficulty speaking English, people in complex households, and people living in nonstandard housing units.[7] Thus one is tempted to conclude that the data from a coverage survey can provide an incredibly accurate measure of census undercount.

Barriers to Measuring Undercount with a Survey

Before drawing that conclusion, however, we must consider a much less incredible interpretation: the differences between the coverage survey and the original census may not represent net undercount as much as they represent the difficulty of matching individual records between two surveys. At a very broad level of aggregation, this methodological difficulty can produce results that look very much like net undercount because the population groups that are hard to match between surveys are generally the same groups that are hard to count. It is only by considering the tremendous barriers to measuring undercount accurately and by examining the detailed findings of the 1990 PES that we are led to accept this alternate

6. Howard Hogan, "The 1990 Post-Enumeration Survey: Operations and Results," *Journal of the American Statistical Association*, 88(423): 1047–60, 1993.

7. Manuel de la Puente, U.S. Bureau of the Census, "Why Are People Missed or Erroneously Included by the Census? A Summary of Findings from Ethnographic Coverage Reports," report prepared for the Advisory Committee for the Design of the Year 2000 Census Meeting, March 5, 1993. J. Gregory Robinson and Edward L. Kobilarcik, U.S. Bureau of the Census, "Identifying Differential Undercounts at Local Geographic Levels: A Targeting Database Approach," paper presented at the Annual Meeting of the Population Association of America, April 1995.

interpretation. If this interpretation is correct, it has very clear implications for how the next census should be conducted: adjusting the new census based on a coverage survey would negate the findings from 100 million census forms based on a statistical artifact.

Two Impossible Tasks. For a coverage survey to measure net undercount with anything approaching an acceptable level of accuracy, it must accomplish two impossible tasks. The impossibility of these tasks should lead us to question its validity even if it appears on the surface to provide a good measure of undercount. In particular, we should not conclude that the Census Bureau has accomplished the impossible merely on the basis of plausible results for the broadest national aggregation. If the detailed results do not make sense as well, then it is untenable to suggest that undercount has been measured with a high level of precision.

The first impossible task that a coverage survey must accomplish is to secure participation by two particularly problematic components of the population that are not counted well by the census: homeless people and people who do not want to be counted. Each census includes a major effort to count people in shelters and on the streets, but it undoubtedly misses a large portion of this population. A coverage survey is not well equipped to measure this component of the undercount, because many homeless people are not likely to be found in the same place a few weeks or months later when the survey is conducted. The Census Bureau understands the impossibility of matching homeless people with their census forms, and *therefore the 1990 PES did not even attempt to address this portion of the undercount.*[8]

A coverage survey does not fare much better with the other problematic component of the population. It is

---

8. Hogan, "The 1990 Post-Enumeration Survey."

hard to imagine that very many of the people who avoided being counted by the census are likely to be counted by a second survey that has essentially the same limitations. If drug dealers, fugitives, and illegal immigrants were afraid to fill out the census form that everyone in the nation was supposed to receive, they are not likely to step forward a few weeks or months later when their households are singled out for visits by another government enumerator. On the contrary, they are likely to avoid the coverage survey even more studiously than they avoided the census. Thus we cannot believe that a coverage survey provides a good measure of undercount unless we are first willing to believe that somehow—without the tools necessary to do so—it manages to secure participation by these two groups of people who were not well counted by the census.

If a coverage survey misses many of the same people who were missed by the census, then the only way it can suggest a plausible level of undercount is by identifying other people as missed by the census when they really were counted. This leads us to the second impossible task that a coverage survey must accomplish: achieving a practically perfect replication and matching of census results for that vast majority of the population which is counted correctly the first time. The problem is that for every hundred people missed by a census there are about 3,000 people who were counted and can therefore mistakenly be identified as missed. These 3,000 people will inevitably include a certain number of challenging cases involving aliases, language barriers, individuals and households that have moved, people with no stable place of residence, and a host of other difficulties. It does not take a large error rate in classifying these 3,000 people who were correctly counted by the census to completely invalidate the attempt to count the 100 people who were missed—especially since many of the people who were missed are making every effort to be missed again.

A hypothetical example will help to demonstrate that even a 99 percent level of accuracy is not sufficient. Let us suppose that the next census has an undercount of 3 percent and an overcount of 1 percent, for a net undercount of 2 percent. Let us also assume that the next coverage survey somehow manages to identify all the people who are missed by the census and all the people who are counted twice or counted in error. This is a very generous assumption, since we have already seen that we have good reason to believe that this is an impossible task. Finally, let us assume that the coverage survey achieves 99 percent accuracy in classifying the individuals who were counted by the census.

The apparent undercount will then include that 3 percent of the population that had been missed by the census, plus nearly another 1 percent that had actually been counted correctly. This is because 1 percent of the 97 percent *not* missed by the census will be falsely identified as undercounted because we achieve "only" 99 percent accuracy in replicating and matching the census results. Thus, even under these unrealistically favorable assumptions, about 25 percent of the apparent undercount will actually represent classification error.[9] The measure of overcount will be even more problematic: it will include that 1 percent of the population that had actually been overcounted, plus nearly another 1 percent that had been counted correctly the first time. This means that about 50 percent of the apparent overcount will actu-

---

9. Expressed as a proportion of the actual population, the people counted by the census who are misclassified as uncounted in this hypothetical example will be $(1.00 - .03) * (1.00 - .99) = .0097$, where .03 is the assumed rate of undercount and .99 is the assumed level of accuracy. If we assume that all of the actual undercount will be detected through the coverage survey, the total estimate of undercount will be $.03 + .0097 = .0397$. Expressed as a proportion of the identified undercount, the people who are misclassified as uncounted will therefore be $.0097 / .0397 = .2443$, or approximately 25 percent.

ally represent classification error.[10] This would hardly be a firm basis for fine-tuning the census count.

This statistical phenomenon is further illustrated by the following example.

Why the Word "American" Is Abbreviated in Census Questions. Whenever one is trying to measure a small component of the population—such as people who have been missed by the census—serious problems can be caused by even very small errors in classifying that vast majority of the population which is not part of the group being measured.

This principle is illustrated by one of the problems that the Census Bureau found while it was testing different ways of asking its new Hispanic-origin question for the 1980 Census. A very small number of people with no Mexican heritage thought that the category "Mexican or Mexican-American" meant "Mexican or American." Since they were "American," they thought that this category applied to them. Unfortunately, since people of Mexican heritage represented only about 4 percent of the national population, even this very small error among the remaining 96 percent of the population was enough to completely invalidate the count of Mexican-Americans. In fact, for many areas, a *majority* of the people selecting this category were found to be Americans with no Mexican heritage.

The 1980 Census therefore used the abbreviation

---

10. Expressed as a proportion of the actual population, the people counted by the census who are misclassified as counted in error will be $(1.00 - .03) * (1.00 - .99) = .0097$, where .03 is the assumed rate of undercount and .99 is the assumed level of accuracy. If we assume that all of the actual overcount will be detected through the coverage survey, the total estimate of overcount will be $.01 + .0097 = .0197$. Expressed as a proportion of the estimated overcount, the people who are misclassified as counted in error will therefore be $.0097 / .0197 = .4924$, or approximately 50 percent.

"Mexican or Mexican-Amer." This was a big improvement, but the 1980 Post-Enumeration Survey found that non-Mexicans still represented a majority of the people choosing this category in some areas with a very low population of Mexican-Americans. The 1990 Census therefore used the category "Mexican or Mexican-Am." This cleared up the problem. These abbreviations are not needed to save space; they are needed to save the data.

A very similar difficulty arises when one tries to measure undercount with a coverage survey. It is sometimes very hard to match up the people that were counted in the coverage survey with the people that were counted in the census. When a mistake is made, people can be counted as missed by the census or as mistakenly included in the census when they really were not. Since there are about ninety-seven of these potential mistakes for every three people who were really missed by the census, even a very low error rate is enough to completely invalidate the measure of undercount. Unfortunately, although the problem is very similar, the solution is not: errors in matching surveys cannot be prevented by anything as simple as using more abbreviations.

Operational Barriers to Accurate Measurement. A coverage survey must therefore achieve far more than 99 percent accuracy in classifying the people who are correctly counted by the census. But is it possible to achieve such a high level of accuracy? Even for simple surveys conducted under ideal conditions, a 99 percent level of accuracy would be impressive. Unfortunately, the census and the coverage survey are not simple, and they are not conducted under ideal conditions. The attempt to match the results of these two surveys must contend with a wide array of daunting problems:

- illegible handwriting
- similarity of names

- use of different nicknames and other variations on names in different surveys
- names that do not have a consistent spelling in the English alphabet
- use of aliases by illegal immigrants, fugitives, and others who place a very high value on privacy; some people have more than one alias, some may use different names on different surveys, and some may be known to neighbors by names that are different from the ones used on the census
- irregular living arrangements, complex households, and households with unstable membership
- differences that arise from collecting most census information through written forms and collecting information for the coverage survey through personal interviews
- households and individuals that move between the census and the coverage survey; this is particularly a problem for college students, recent graduates from high school or college, and people who migrate between northern and southern states on a seasonal basis; many of these people move within a few weeks after the April census
- differences that arise from having different household members provide information for the different surveys, or from having a responsible household member provide information for the census and a child, neighbor, or landlord provide information for the coverage survey; (for example, differences in the reported name, age, race, or marital status can make it difficult to determine whether a person found by the coverage survey is really the same person found by the census; this problem was compounded in 1990 because the survey to measure undercount was centered on the Fourth of July weekend and the survey to measure "erroneous enumerations" was centered on the Thanksgiving weekend; it is obviously difficult to survey a college town during Thanksgiving week to determine who was living there the previous April)
- language barriers; these are a particularly serious

problem for a coverage survey because it relies on personal interviews instead of on a written survey that respondents can complete with help from friends or other family members

- people who are included in the census but avoid inclusion in the coverage survey because they do not want to be identified by government authorities
- homeless or transient people who are enumerated in one housing unit by the census but are in a different housing unit or on the streets at the time of the coverage survey
- homeless or transient people who are enumerated in the streets by the census but are found in a housing unit by the coverage survey
- information that is fabricated by the enumerator or by the respondent
- clerical errors and processing errors
- failure to follow complex procedures precisely
- census forms that are coded to the wrong geographic area, making it impossible to match them with the proper survey results
- people who give an inaccurate response when they are asked where the members of their household were living on April Fools Day

These problems are more than just hypothetical illustrations: many of them have been documented and quantified by analysts from the Census Bureau and elsewhere, who confirm that the undercount analysis involves very serious levels of matching error and other error. (See chapter 3 in this volume.) Thus, in addition to knowing from logical arguments and hypothetical illustrations that serious problems are inevitable, we know from experience that serious problems actually do occur.

In place of our previous assumptions that a coverage survey measures overcount and undercount perfectly and that it matches the correct findings of the census with 99 percent accuracy, we should therefore consider the implications of a somewhat more modest level of success. Let's say that the next coverage survey identifies 30 percent of the actual undercount and 40 percent of the actual overcount, that the undercount analysis averages an impressive 96.2 percent rate of accuracy in replicating and matching the correct results of the census, and that the overcount analysis averages a similarly impressive 97.3 percent rate of accuracy. Although classification error would then account for an overwhelming 80 percent of the people identified as undercounted and 87 percent of the people identified as overcounted, the estimated net undercount at the national level would be the same 1.6 percent that was suggested by the coverage survey for 1990.[11] In other words, the estimate of undercount would primarily reflect errors in matching survey responses with census responses, yet the broadest national estimate of net undercount would appear very plausible.

Evidence of Error in the Survey

To people who are interested only in the national count of total population, the hypothetical example above may

---

11. Expressed as a proportion of the actual population, the people counted by the census who are misclassified as uncounted in this hypothetical example will be $(1.00 - .03) * (1.00 - .962) = .03686$, where .03 is the assumed rate of undercount and .962 is the assumed level of accuracy. If we assume that 30 percent of the actual undercount will be detected through the coverage survey, the total estimate of undercount will be $(.03 * .30) + .03686 = .04586$. Expressed as a proportion of the identified undercount, the people who are misclassified as uncounted will therefore be $.03686 / .04586 = .8038$, or approximately 80 percent.

The people counted by the census who are misclassified as counted in error will be $(1.00 - .03) * (1.00 - .973) = .02619$, and the total estimate of overcount will be $(.01 * .40) + .02619 = .03019$. Expressed as a proportion of the identified overcount, the people who are misclassified as counted in error will therefore be $.02619 / .03019 = .8675$, or approximately 87 percent. The estimate of net undercount will be $.04586 - .03019 = .01567$, or 1.6 percent.

not appear very troubling. After all, since this example assumes that the errors in measuring undercount are largely offset by the errors in measuring overcount, the resulting national population total is actually closer to the assumed true population than is the unadjusted census count. What makes this example troubling is the fact that the undercount adjustments are relied on for far more than a national population total. They purport to tell us which segments of the population and which parts of the country are undercounted more than others. The critical point that needs to be understood is that, if the coverage survey really does fail to measure a large portion of the undercount and if it mistakenly identifies people as missed by the census who really were not, then the differential undercounts it suggests will be misleading. They will largely reflect differences in the amount of error in measuring undercount rather than differences in the amount of undercount itself. What would we expect such adjustments to look like? To put it simply, we would expect them to look just like adjustments developed from the 1990 Post-Enumeration Survey. (See figure 2–2 and table 2–2 below.)

Comparison with Results of Demographic Analysis. At the national level, it would not be surprising for the under-count adjustments to look fairly reasonable: since the population groups that are hard to match between two surveys are generally the same groups that are hard to count in the census, we would expect the findings for very broad components of the population to be at least roughly similar to the results of the Census Bureau's "demographic analysis" method. Of course they would not be identical, since the level of difficulty in matching each group between surveys does not correspond precisely to the level of difficulty in counting it for the census. For example, some problems such as language barriers and aliases pose more difficulty in survey-matching than in taking a census,

27

FIGURE 2–2

BASIS OF UNDERCOUNT ESTIMATES FOR THE 1990 CENSUS

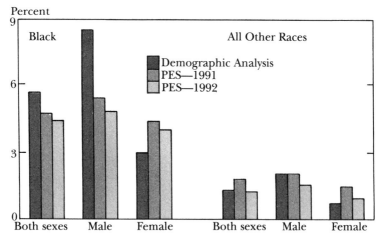

TABLE 2–2

ALTERNATE ESTIMATES OF UNDERCOUNT FOR THE 1990 CENSUS

(percent)

Race and Sex	Demographic Analysis	Post-Enumeration Survey	
		June 1991 Revision	Sept. 1992 Revision
Black			
Both sexes	5.7	4.8	4.4
Male	8.5	5.4	4.9
Female	3.0	4.3	4.0
All Other Races			
Both sexes	1.3	1.7	1.2
Male	2.0	2.0	1.5
Female	0.6	1.4	0.9

SOURCE: The undercount estimates based on the PES are from Barbara Everitt Bryant, "Census-Taking for a Litigious, Data-Driven Society," *Chance: New Directions for Statistics and Computing,* vol. 6, no. 3, 1993. The estimates based on demographic analysis are from U.S. Department of Commerce, "Census Bureau Releases Refined 1990 Census Coverage Estimates from Demographic Analysis," Press Release of June 13, 1991, table 1.

28

and segments of the population that are counted very well in the census are at the greatest risk of having classification error exceed the actual level of undercount.

Thus, while advocates of adjustment have not considered the pattern of differences displayed in figure 2–2 to be unreasonable, the final national PES results for 1990 are actually quite different from the estimates based on demographic analysis even for very broad population groups. The apparent undercount for black males is 42 percent less than the rate suggested by demographic analysis, and the rate for white, Native American, and Asian/Pacific females is 50 percent higher. Under most circumstances, these differences would be considered very substantial. They provide clear confirmation of the theoretical analysis presented earlier in this chapter. Many of the people missed by the census are evidently missed by the survey as well, while a huge proportion of those classified as missed by the census are people who really had not been missed at all.

Errors in Individual Measurements of Undercount. We would expect an even worse situation below the national level. If the measure of net undercount is more sensitive to variations in the rate of classification error and other survey problems than to variations in the actual rate of undercount, it would not be surprising to find some serious deviations from the orderly pattern that would be found in the near-perfect analysis that is required. For example, it would not be surprising for the adjustment factors to look something like the ones displayed in table 2–3.

Table 2–3 shows some of the initial undercount measurements for children under age ten that the Census Bureau developed based on the 1990 PES. This age group was chosen for this analysis because there is no obvious reason to expect householders to misreport their young male children at a significantly different rate from their young female children. It is therefore disconcerting that there are some very large differences between the apparent undercount rates for boys and girls in this age group. In fact, these eighteen pairs of figures were selected for the table because each involves a discrepancy of *more than ten percentage points.*

It is even more disconcerting that these differences follow no discernible pattern. Sometimes the rate for boys is higher, but sometimes the rate for girls is higher. In one place black renters have a higher rate for boys, but in another place they have a higher rate for girls. In some places the gender discrepancy for whites is similar to the gender discrepancy for blacks, but in other places it is the opposite. Sometimes one race category in a large city seems to have a higher undercount for boys, but another race in the same city seems to have a higher undercount for girls. It is not surprising when signs of estimation error are visible for small components of the population in small geographic areas, but here we see apparently arbitrary figures for even the largest population groups in some of the largest cities and across entire regions. Thus, the undercount rates in table 2–3 suggest a high level of measurement error rather than the high level of precision required for an adequate adjustment to the census.[12]

The PES findings in table 2–3 provide a good basis for testing whether we can trust a coverage survey when it tells us that some population groups have higher undercounts than others. We have seen that these apparent un-

---

12. There are several types of measurement error. Although the point being made here is that the large amount of error in the adjustments is consistent with the thesis that large amounts of *non-sampling* error are inevitable, it should be noted that *sampling* error is also a very serious problem for the undercount adjustments. Actually, there is more than enough error to go around: these adjustments can reflect a very large amount of sampling error as well as a very large amount of non-sampling error. For purposes of data quality, both types of error are very problematic.

dercounts seem to be implausible, but that by itself does not prove that they did not happen. If we can confirm that these differential undercounts did take place, then the credibility of coverage surveys as a tool for measuring undercount will be greatly increased. Conversely, if it can be demonstrated that they did not take place, then the credibility of coverage surveys will be lost. If a coverage survey can indicate large undercount differentials where they do not exist, then it is obviously not a very reliable tool for measuring undercount.

Fortunately, because the ratio of male to female children is one of the most stable of all demographic statistics, these adjustment factors can be tested quite definitively. For each of the nation's nine regions, 51 percent of the young children enumerated in the 1990 Census were boys and 49 percent were girls. Likewise, for each of the major race categories, 51 percent of the young children enumerated were boys and 49 percent were girls. Among the nation's 284 metropolitan areas and consolidated metropolitan areas, the percentage of young children who were boys varied very little, ranging from a low of 50.3 percent in Pine Bluff, Arkansas, to a high of 52.1 percent in Topeka, Kansas. Therefore, if the large differential undercounts indicated in table 2–3 really did take place, they should be very obvious. Boys should represent less than 51 percent of the total for areas with a large undercount of boys, but they should represent more than 51 percent of the total for areas with a large undercount of girls. Furthermore, if the undercounts indicated by the coverage survey really did take place, we should expect each area to move closer to the norm after it is "corrected" for census undercount.

In fact, however, we find just the opposite. Table 2–4 shows that the percentage of children under age ten who are boys is about the same not only in each region, each race, and each metropolitan area, but also in the areas for which the coverage survey found large undercount differ-

31

TABLE 2–3

SELECTED UNDERCOUNT MEASUREMENTS FOR CHILDREN UNDER AGE TEN FROM THE 1990 POST-ENUMERATION SURVEY

Region	Area Type	Tenure	Race	*Apparent Undercount, %*	
				Male	Female
Pacific	Noncentral cities	Renter/ owner	Asian/Pacific	5	17
Mid-Atlantic	Central cities in New York City PMSA	Renter/ owner	Asian/Pacific	25	9
East North Central	Central cities in metro areas w/ central city >250K	Owner	Black	26	15
Pacific	Central cities in Los Angeles PMSA	Owner	Black	28	8
Mid-Atlantic	Central cities in New York City PMSA	Owner	Black	0	23
South Atlantic	Central cities in metro areas w/ central city >250K	Renter	Black	26	16
Pacific	Central cities in Los Angeles PMSA	Renter	Black	20	10
Pacific	Noncentral cities	Renter/ owner	Black	31	6
Mid-Atlantic	Noncentral cities in metro areas w/ central city >250K	Renter/ owner	Hispanic (except black)	2	16

Region	Description	Tenure	Race/ethnicity		
Mid-Atlantic	All central cities	Renter/ owner	Hispanic (except black)	14	2
West South Central	Central cities in Houston, Dallas, and Fort Worth PMSAs	Renter/ owner	Hispanic (except black)	8	19
South Atlantic	All nonmetro areas and all noncentral cities	Renter/ owner	Hispanic (except black)	9	22
West South Central	Central cities in metro areas w/ central city >250K	Renter	White, Native Am., and Asian/Pacific except Hisp.	−5	11
East North Central	Central cities in metro areas w/ central city >250K	Renter	White, Native Am., and Asian/Pacific except Hisp.	21	4
East North Central	Central cities in Detroit and Chicago PMSAs	Renter	White, Native Am., and Asian/Pacific except Hisp.	−4	14
West South Central	Central cities in Houston, Dallas, and Fort Worth PMSAs	Renter	White, Native Am., and Asian/Pacific except Hisp.	7	21
South Atlantic	Central cities in metro areas w/o central city >250K	Renter/ owner	White, Native Am., and Asian/Pacific except Hisp.	10	−1
South Atlantic	Nonmetro areas except places >10K	Renter/ owner	White, Native Am., and Asian/Pacific except Hisp.	3	16

SOURCE: U.S. Department of Commerce, Bureau of the Census, unpublished file dated June 14, 1991, containing adjustment factors derived from the 1990 Post-Enumeration Survey, prior to application of a statistical smoothing procedure. These adjustment factors reflect the amount of apparent net undercount actually measured in the PES sample for the indicated geographic areas and demographic groups.

entials between boys and girls. It is only after applying these adjustments derived from the coverage survey that serious anomalies are found. As shown by figure 2–3, the percentage of children who are boys deviates dramatically from the norm after adjustment. Even though Pine Bluff and Topeka are "outliers" among the nation's metropolitan areas, the adjusted census counts are *two to six times* as far from the norm as Pine Bluff and Topeka. Thus, these "undercounts" measured in the PES sample do not correspond at all to actual undercounts in the areas that the sample represents. The census is not really broken until after it is fixed.

The point here is not merely that the 1990 coverage survey produced faulty undercount measurements for young boys and girls. The problem is much broader than that, since the difficulties discussed in this chapter apply just as much to other age groups as to children, and just as much to other demographic characteristics as to the sex ratio. The foregoing analysis focuses on the sex ratio of children merely because sex ratios provide a convenient and definitive basis for demonstrating the implausibility of the undercount measurements below the age where school attendance, military service, and employment patterns cause different communities to have a different mixture of males and females. The focus on the sex ratio of young children should not by any means imply that undercount measurements are worse for this age group or that they would affect sex ratios more than the other population and housing characteristics that are measured by the census. In the absence of any known problem that would scramble the undercount measurements for boys and girls without affecting the figures for other age groups and other demographic characteristics, we have to suspect that the measurements are faulty in other respects as well. The point is therefore nothing less than this: because the large undercount differentials shown in table 2–3 are clearly spurious, we cannot trust a coverage survey to tell us which segments of the population have higher undercounts than others.

Do Errors Make a Difference?

It may take a few moments to comprehend the effect that adjustment factors like those displayed in table 2–3 would have if they were applied to the census.[13] To those of us who have become accustomed to census data that generally make sense at the local level, it is mind-boggling to consider the prospect of largely arbitrary adjustments—and sometimes arbitrarily large ones—applied to every number in the census. In an effort to address a relatively small inaccuracy at the national level, we would utterly destroy the reliability of census data at the state and local levels.

Perhaps most alarming is the effect on comparisons over time. If coverage surveys can indicate large differential undercounts between boys and girls even where no differences exist, they can also indicate large differential

---

13. The adjustment factors in table 2–3 reflect the amount of apparent net undercount actually measured in the PES sample for the indicated geographic areas and demographic groups. It should be noted that these factors were subsequently subjected to a statistical "smoothing" procedure to produce new factors that followed a more consistent pattern by age, race, and sex. It was these smoothed factors that were actually proposed in 1991 for use in adjusting the 1990 Census. Further modifications proposed in 1992 for use in adjusting the population base for population estimates would have combined males and females under age seventeen. The resulting collapsed adjustment factors represent the Census Bureau's latest official estimate of undercount in the 1990 Census. The smoothed adjustment factors would be appropriate for use in estimating the practical effect of adjusting the 1990 Census data for undercount. The nonsmoothed adjustment factors are pertinent for the current analysis, since they reflect the amount of apparent undercount actually identified by the PES. The nonsmoothed factors are also relevant in the context of Census 2000, since the Census Bureau does not plan to use a statistical smoothing process in the next Census. The question of smoothing is discussed further in chapter 3.

TABLE 2–4

BEFORE ADJUSTMENT FOR UNDERCOUNT: CONSISTENT DATA ON CHILDREN WHO ARE BOYS, IN PERCENT, 1990

Data from Enumeration		Selected Areas for which the PES Indicated a Large Differential Undercount between Boys and Girls	
U.S. Total	51	1. Asians/Pacific Islanders in noncentral cities of the Pacific Region	51
Race Categories		2. Asians/Pacific Islanders in central cities of the New York City PMSA	52
White	51	3. Blacks in noncentral cities of the Pacific Region	51
Black	51	4. Hispanics in noncentral cities of large MSAs in the Mid-Atlantic Region	51
Native American	51	5. Hispanics in central cities of the Mid-Atlantic Region	51
Asian/Pacific	51	6. Hispanics in central cities of the Houston, Dallas, and Fort Worth PMSAs	51
Other race	51		
Hispanic	51		
Regions			
New England	51		
Middle Atlantic	51		

East North Central	51
West North Central	51
South Atlantic	51
East South Central	51
West South Central	51
Mountain	51
Pacific	51

Extremes Out of 284 Metro Areas:

Lowest: Pine Bluff, Arkansas	50.3
Highest: Topeka, Kansas	52.1

7. Hispanics in noncentral cities or nonmetropolitan areas of the South Atlantic Region	51
8. Non-Hispanic whites, Native Americans, and Asians/Pacific Islanders in central cities of small MSAs in the South Atlantic region	51
9. Non-Hispanic whites, Native Americans, and Asians/Pacific Islanders in nonmetropolitan areas of the South Atlantic region (excluding places with over 10,000 persons)	51

Source: The percentage of children who are boys was calculated based on the 1990 Census of Population and Housing, U.S. Department of Commerce, Bureau of the Census, Summary Tape File 1-C. Because census counts by age, race, sex, and tenure have not been published, this table does not include the nine segments of the population in table 2–3 that involve only renters or only homeowners. Although the race distinctions that are made in Summary Tape File 1-C do not correspond precisely to the race distinctions on which the undercount adjustments were calculated, these discrepancies involve a very small number of people and they do not significantly affect the present analysis. Black Hispanics are counted as Hispanic in STF 1-C, but they should not be included with other Hispanics for purposes of analyzing the undercount adjustments. Likewise, Asians/Pacific Islanders of Hispanic origin are counted as Asians/Pacific Islanders in STF 1-C, but they should not be included with that group for purposes of analyzing the undercount adjustments.

FIGURE 2–3
AFTER ADJUSTMENT FOR UNDERCOUNT: DRAMATIC VARIATIONS
IN PERCENTAGE OF CHILDREN WHO ARE BOYS, 1990

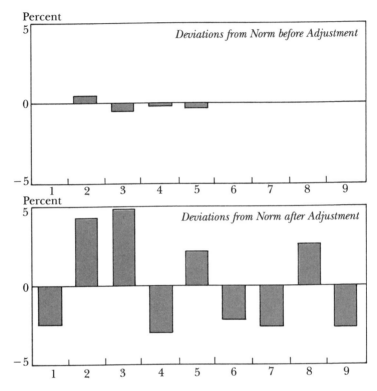

NOTES: 1. Asians/Pacific Islanders in non-central cities of the Pacific Region, 49; 2. Asians/Pacific Islanders in central cities of the New York City PMSA, 55; 3. Blacks in noncentral cities of the Pacific Region, 56; 4. Hispanics in noncentral cities of large MSAs in the Mid-Atlantic Region, 48; 5. Hispanics in central cities of the Mid-Atlantic Region, 53; 6. Hispanics in central cities of the Houston, Dallas, and Fort Worth PMSA's, 49; 7. Hispanics in noncentral cities or non-metropolitan areas of the South Atlantic Region, 48; 8. Non-Hispanic whites, Native Americans, and Asians/Pacific Islanders in central cities of small MSAs in the South Atlantic region, 54; 9. Non-Hispanic whites, Native Americans, and Asians/Pacific Islanders in nonmetropolitan areas of the South Atlantic region (excluding places with over 10,000 persons), 48.
SOURCE: The data were calculated after applying the adjustment factors from table 2–3 to census counts from Summary Tape File 1-C.

38

undercounts between one census and the next where no differences exist. To illustrate the potential implications of this problem, let us consider what would happen if there turns out to be no real difference in certain under-count rates for Census 2000 and Census 2010, but the cov-erage surveys indicate the same spurious differences between these two years that the 1990 PES found between boys and girls. Under these assumptions, the numbers in table 2–3 could all remain the same,[14] but they would rep-resent spurious undercount differentials between Census 2000 and Census 2010 instead of spurious undercount dif-ferentials between boys and girls in 1990. This would gen-erate many interesting demographic "findings":

• The counts of Asians/Pacific Islanders in noncentral cities of the Pacific region would be inflated by 5 percent in 2000 but by 17 percent in 2010. (See line 1 of table 2–3.) The adjusted censuses would therefore suggest far greater growth in the number of Asians than actually oc-curred. What effect would this have on attitudes toward Asian immigrants in these communities?

• The count of black homeowners in central cities of the Los Angeles PMSA would be inflated by 28 percent in 2000 but by only 8 percent in 2010. Similarly, the count of black renters would be inflated by 20 percent in 2000 and by 10 percent in 2010. (See lines 4 and 7 of table 2–3.) The adjusted census data would therefore show a large exodus of the black population and a substantial drop in black home ownership for Los Angeles relative to the ac-tual trend. What effect would this have on race relations?

---

14. Our assumption that "the undercount adjustments indicate the same spurious *differences* between these two times that the 1990 PES found between boys and girls" does not require the adjustments them-selves to be the same as the 1990 adjustments for boys and girls, but merely for the differences to be the same. The numbers could remain the same, but they would not necessarily have to. For simplicity and clarity of presentation, the illustrations are based on the special case in which the adjustments are the same.

What would be the effect on government housing programs and antidiscrimination programs?

- The count of black homeowners in central cities of the New York City PMSA, conversely, would be inflated by 0 percent in 2000 and by 23 percent in 2010. (See line 5 of table 2–3.) This area would therefore seem to have a dramatic rise in black home ownership relative to the actual trend. Of course, home ownership would not by any means be the only variable affected by these faulty adjustment factors: poverty, marital status, and every other characteristic correlated with race and with home ownership would also be affected. Social scientists could spend the decade trying to explain why the economic status of blacks seemed to rise so rapidly in New York City while it seemed to decline in Los Angeles. What would be the effect on the credibility of the census when they discovered the answer?

- The counts of white, Native American, and Asian/Pacific renters in Detroit and Chicago would be *decreased* by 5 percent in 2000, but they would be inflated by 11 percent in 2010. Thus there would seem to be a dramatic increase in renters and a shift away from home ownership in these cities relative to the actual trend. (See line 15 of table 2–3.) In contrast, other central cities in these same metropolitan areas would have their counts for these demographic categories inflated by 21 percent in 2000 and by only 4 percent in 2010. (See line 14 of table 2–3.) The faulty adjustment factors would therefore make it appear that huge numbers of white renters had moved from Detroit and Chicago to other nearby central cities before 2000, but that they moved back in the next decade.

Of course, these illustrations are only hypothetical. Perhaps Los Angeles will have reasonable undercount adjustments for black homeowners in 2000 and 2010. Maybe its adjusted census data will show a spurious decline in its elderly population instead, and maybe it will be New York that shows a spurious decline in black home ownership. We will not know before it happens. Even worse, we will not know even *after* it happens. When adjusted census data suggest a dramatic change in population trends, we will not know how much of the change represents actual demographic shifts and how much represents spurious differences in undercount adjustments. Are we ready to discover dramatic new (and totally false) trends in disease prevalence, mortality rates, school enrollment, income distribution, housing patterns, marital status, welfare dependency, gender differences, and all the other issues that are studied on the basis of census data? We expect a census to increase our knowledge about population trends, but an adjustment methodology that can indicate large differentials where differentials do not exist would increase our ignorance instead.

Conclusion

We cannot escape the conclusion that the method proposed for correcting census undercount has some rather serious shortcomings. The effect on the validity of the 1990 Census would have been devastating, and we can expect the effect on Census 2000 to be similar: the problems are attributable not to minor flaws in methodology or implementation, but rather to the impossibility of measuring undercount through the proposed coverage survey. Unless we can convince people who do not want to be counted to answer our surveys, and unless we can replicate and match the valid census results with near-perfect accuracy, any undercount estimates that are developed in this manner will be dominated by measurement error. Instead of describing variations in the amount of undercount from one area to another, they will largely describe variations in the amount of error in replicating the census and in matching individuals identified by the survey with individuals identified by the census. Once the impossibility of the task is recognized, one can only be impressed by how close the Census Bureau seemed to come to succeeding in 1990. One must also be impressed, however, by how close we are to destroying the credibility and the value of the census.

3

Quantifying Measurement Error and Bias in the 1990 Undercount Adjustments

The opening pages of chapter 2 in this volume set up a paradox: since the number of people who want to avoid being identified by the government is more than sufficient to account for the level of undercount identified through demographic analysis, and since many of these people can be relied on to avoid the coverage survey as well as the census, how is it that the 1990 coverage survey suggests about the right level of total undercount at the national level?

The solution I have proposed is that this tendency to miss many of the same people in both the coverage survey and the census—a phenomenon that statisticians refer to as "correlation bias"—is offset by counting some people as missed by the census when they really were included. I have suggested that rather than just reflecting undercount, the undercount factors derived from the coverage survey reflect a variety of methodological difficulties involving imperfect replication of the census, survey matching, unreliable interviews, geocoding problems, and the like.

Chapter 2 demonstrates that this is a plausible solution to the paradox and that it is consistent with both the plausible undercount estimates at the national level and the implausible estimates for the individual segments of the population for which adjustment factors were calculated, known as *poststrata*. The chapter shows that, although an extremely high level of accuracy is required for an adequate measure of undercount, the obstacles to an accurate coverage survey are immense. It points out many specific types of error that are difficult or impossible to avoid, and it shows that the proposed undercount adjustments for 1990 were suggestive of high levels of error.

Even these limited accomplishments of chapter 2 are significant. Proponents of the proposed undercount adjustment are left with the task of explaining how the 1990 coverage survey could indicate very large and demonstrably spurious differential undercounts for young children. In addition, they must explain how we can rely on the 5 percent, 10 percent, and 20 percent differential undercounts identified between other segments of the population when the 5 percent, 10 percent, and 20 percent differential undercounts identified between young boys and girls are known to be spurious. Proponents of the undercount adjustment must make a believable argument that the coverage survey somehow really did count critical groups of people who were missed by the 1990 census— for example, homeless people and the illegal immigrants, drug dealers, fugitives, and others who do not want the government to know where they are. The Census Bureau must demonstrate either that it achieved extremely low error rates in the face of seemingly insurmountable obstacles, or else that—notwithstanding the demonstrated inaccuracies of the undercount measurements for some individual segments of the population—it has enough luck and skill to ensure that large errors will offset each other very precisely. Merely a general tendency for errors to offset one another is not enough: an extremely high level of accuracy is required to measure a phenomenon as small and elusive as census undercount at the subnational level. Each of these issues is critical to the success of the effort to measure undercount. The credibility of the proposed method cannot be restored unless its proponents are successful on all these points.

A major limitation of chapter 2 is that although it suggests what sorts of errors are difficult or impossible to avoid, it stops short of showing that those errors actually occurred or how serious they were. To fill this gap in the analysis, chapter 3 relies on evaluation studies by the Census Bureau and the work of other analysts. That work confirms that the errors are very large indeed and that they did not offset each other precisely in the analysis of the 1990 coverage survey.

The Census Bureau has extensively evaluated the process and results of the 1990 coverage survey, which is commonly referred to as the Post-Enumeration Survey (PES). Its findings are written up in twenty-two unpublished reports, eight of which are referenced in this chapter. These reports, which are known as the P-project reports, were issued in July 1991 under the main title "1990 Post-Enumeration Survey Evaluation Project." The reports are referred to in this chapter by their number within the series—for example, P-4 or P-16. Most of the references to these reports and many of the other quantitative observations that appear below are based on the work of Professor Leo Breiman, an emeritus professor of statistics at the University of California, Berkeley.[1]

Six major sources of error are quantified below: matching error, fabrication of interviews, ambiguity or misreporting of usual residence, geocoding errors, unreliable interviews, and the number of unresolved cases. It will be shown that the level of error and uncertainty contributed by each of these factors is very substantial relative to the magnitude of net undercount. Thus each of these error sources by itself is sufficient to demonstrate that the sort of coverage survey used by the Census Bureau is not

---

1. Leo Breiman, "The 1991 Census Adjustment: Undercount or Bad Data?" *Statistical Science*, 9(4): 458–537 (1994).

capable of accurately measuring census undercount. It will then be shown that the various identified sources of error actually did increase the 1990 undercount estimate enough to explain the paradox.

Matching Error

A critical step in measuring undercount through a coverage survey is to match people counted in the coverage survey with people counted in the census. Most people are counted by both surveys, but problems such as misspellings, misreporting of age, language barriers, aliases, missing data, errors in recording the address, changes in household composition, and a host of other difficulties can make it difficult to match up the records. Any failure to match the records can lead to an overestimate of undercount: the person's record in the Post-Enumeration Survey, sometimes referred to as the P-sample, can be mistakenly counted as having been missed by the census. Yet the person's census response—the census enumerations from the same geographic areas are sometimes referred to as the E-sample—cannot be classified as erroneous unless strict criteria are met.[2] (After all, it is a valid record.) Thus, when records fail to match, it is possible for people to be counted twice. The many barriers to matching the coverage survey results with the census are described in the preceding chapter, and their seriousness is confirmed by the results of the Census Bureau's evaluation studies.

---

2. For example, Howard Hogan, then director of the Undercount Research Staff of the Census Bureau, wrote the following in 1991 in an unpublished Census Bureau paper titled "The 1990 Post-Enumeration Survey: An Overview": "Proving that someone does not exist is not easy. . . . The rules require the interviewer to find at least three knowledgeable respondents in an effort to determine whether an enumeration was fictitious." This would be difficult to do in a case where an unmatched person really existed.

As explained in the P-8 report, a computer-matching process was able to resolve about 75 percent of the P-sample records, and the remaining records went to two independent teams of trained matchers. Although these teams used the same definitions and guidelines, they had a surprisingly high rate of disagreement regarding which people counted by the PES had been counted by the census. Of people classified as "matched" by the first team, 5.7 percent were classified as "not matched" and 4.5 percent were classified as "unresolved" by the second team. Of those classified as "not matched" by the first team, 4.8 percent were classified as "matched" and 1.3 percent were classified as "unresolved" by the second team. Of those classified as "unresolved" by the first team, 22.7 percent were classified as "matched" and 8.0 percent were classified as "unmatched" by the second team.[3] Although the matching process must achieve near-perfection in order to accurately measure the 1 percent or 2 percent of the population that is missed by the census, it is obviously a very difficult task, and even teams using the same guidelines can differ widely in their judgments.

This high level of disagreement has several serious implications:

- First, it indicates that the number of "difficult" cases for which match status is not obvious is very large, greatly exceeding the estimated level of net undercount. This circumstance demonstrates the impossibility of measuring undercount accurately through a coverage survey, even apart from any other considerations.
- Second, since trained teams differ substantially in their judgments, it follows that some of the judgments reached by the final team of matchers are likely to be wrong: some of the people counted by the census will be

---

3. Michael Ringwelski, *P-8 Report: Matching Error—Estimates of Clerical Error from Quality Assurance Results*, U.S. Bureau of the Census, 1990 Post-Enumeration Survey Evaluation Project, Series #I-2 (1991).

47

identified as missed, some of the people missed by the census will be identified as counted, some of the people counted correctly by the census will be identified as counted in error, and some of the people counted in error will be identified as counted correctly. If the number of difficult cases were small, we could hope that the errors would come close to canceling each other out. However, given the high level of disagreement between the matching teams, any of these types of error could potentially exceed the actual level of undercount: "close" is therefore not enough.

• Third, since the matching process obviously involves high levels of subjectivity and art, it is subject to additional sources of bias. Will the match rate be different if the cases are examined in the first week of matching or in the final week? Will the match rate be different depending on which regional office examines them? If a difficult case falls into a category that is expected to have a high undercount rate, will that decrease its likelihood of being classified as matched? If a similar case falls into a category that is expected to have a low undercount rate, will that increase its likelihood of being classified as matched? Such issues can have a significant effect on the differential undercount rates of individual segments of the population and of different geographic regions. If matching were an objective process whose results could be fully determined by the Census Bureau's matching rules, these questions would be insignificant. Because the process is obviously a somewhat subjective one, however, these questions become very important. In fact, since the number of difficult cases is quite large and the level of disagreement between teams exceeds the total level of undercount, these questions must be considered critical.

• A fourth implication of the high level of disagreement between different match teams is that the results for a given set of records are likely to be different each time the match is performed. Clear evidence of this is provided by the results of rematching selected blocks that initially had large numbers of nonmatches and erroneously enumerated persons: rematching only 104 out of the 5,290 block clusters resulted in a decrease of 250,000 (about 5 percent) in the estimated net national undercount.[4]

Fabrication of Interviews

Fabricated data is another example of a data collection problem whose magnitude is very substantial relative to the magnitude of census undercount. Many large surveys conducted by the Census Bureau appear to have a significant number of records that are fabricated by the interviewer. Previous research has shown that, overall, between 2 percent and 5 percent of the interviewers are dishonest in their data collection and that between 0.5 percent and 1.5 percent of the interviews themselves are fabricated.[5] One-time surveys such as the census and the PES are particularly vulnerable to this problem, since temporary employees are found to be more likely to fabricate records than permanent employees. Workers who are detected fabricating data sometimes do so on a large scale. It has been found that, on average, inexperienced interviewers who were detected fabricating data did so for 30 percent of the units in their assignment; for more experienced interviewers, the rate was 19 percent.[6]

While the prospect that perhaps 0.5 percent or 1.5

---

4. Howard Hogan, "The 1990 Post-Enumeration Survey: Operations and Results," *Journal of the American Statistical Association,* 88(423): 1047–60 (1993).

5. S. L. Stokes and P. M. Jones, "Evaluation of the Interviewer Quality Control Procedure for the Post-Enumeration Survey," *American Statistical Association 1989 Proceedings of the Section of Survey Research Methods,* 696–98 (1989).

6. P. P. Biemer and S. L. Stokes, "The Optimal Design of Quality Control Samples to Detect Interviewer Cheating," *Journal of Official Statistics,* 5: 23–39 (1989).

percent of the census and PES interviews are fabricated may not sound extremely serious at first, it must be remembered that we are trying to measure a net undercount of only about 1 percent or 2 percent of the population. Thus, instead of saying that 0.5 percent and 1.5 percent are small relative to 100 percent, it is more pertinent to say that they are very substantial relative to 1 percent or 2 percent. (Of course, it should be noted that undercount rates are higher than 1 percent or 2 percent for some demographic groups and some types of area. That circumstance does not greatly affect this comparison, however, since fabrication rates also tend to be highest in the areas that are most difficult to enumerate.)[7]

Both fabrication in the census and fabrication in the PES have very serious implications for estimating undercount. When a block cluster with interviews that were fabricated by a census enumerator is included in the PES, it will raise the rates of undercount and erroneous enumeration for the segments of the population (poststrata) represented within it. Since, as already noted, it is difficult to prove that people do not exist, the increase in the apparent rate of erroneous enumeration may not be as great as the increase in the apparent undercount rate. This would lead to an overestimate of net undercount for these poststrata.

Fabrication within the PES is even more problematic. When people counted by the PES are matched against census questionnaires, any fabricated PES records can look like people who were missed by the census. When the corresponding census records are tested for validity, however, they are likely to be classified as valid: it is partic-

7. Antoinette Tremblay, *P-5 Report: Analysis of PES P-Sample Fabrications from PES Quality Control Data*, U.S. Bureau of the Census, 1990 Post-Enumeration Survey Evaluation Project, Series #E-4 (1991); Kirsten West, *P-6 Report: Fabrication in the P-Sample: Interviewer Effect*, U.S. Bureau of the Census, 1990 Post-Enumeration Survey Evaluation Project, Series #G-2 (1991).

ularly difficult to prove that people do not exist if they really do exist. Thus fabrication once again can lead to an overestimate of net undercount. Fabricated PES records would be particularly difficult to detect in cases where the housing unit was vacant during the census or during PES follow-up.

The actual amount of fabrication in the PES is difficult to determine. The P-5a report, which is based on data that were not specifically designed to detect fabrication, identified only 0.03 percent of the cases in the P-sample evaluation follow-up data as fabrications.[8] These cases were estimated in the P-16 report to have inflated the national undercount estimate by 50,000 persons, or about 1 percent of the total net undercount.[9] The P-5 report, however, used quality control data collected during the PES to identify 0.26 percent of the PES household interviews and 0.06 percent of the remaining cases on a national level as fabrications.[10] Although this is a much lower rate of fabrication than would be expected based on the studies cited above, it is nevertheless about eight times the proportion of cases identified as fabrications in the P-5a report, suggesting that perhaps fabrications represent about 8 percent of the total net undercount. Yet another Census Bureau report on this issue, the P-6 report, was designed to gain knowledge about fabrication that may have been undetected in the quality control operation. This report found that only 39 percent of the interviewers whose match rates were suggestive of high levels of fabrication had been identified in the quality control opera-

---

8. Kirsten K. West, *P-5a Report: Analysis of P-Sample Fabrication from Evaluation Follow-Up Data,* U.S. Bureau of the Census, 1990 Post-Enumeration Survey Evaluation Project, Series #F-1 (1991).

9. Mary H. Mulry, *P-16 Report: Total Error in PES Estimates by Evaluation Post Strata,* U.S. Bureau of the Census, 1990 Post-Enumeration Survey Evaluation Project, Series #R-6 (1991).

10. Tremblay, *P-5 Report: Analysis of PES P-Sample Fabrications.*

tion.[11] That finding suggests that the level of fabrication in the PES may have been close to the level that has been found in other similar surveys, making it a very significant problem indeed.

The P-6 report also found that fabrication rates seemed to vary substantially from one region to another. Interviewers who appeared to have high levels of fabrication accounted for 2 percent to 5 percent of the interviews in most regions, but they accounted for 7.7 percent of the interviews in the Atlanta regional office and 8.8 percent of the interviews in the Denver regional office.[12] Regional variation in the amount of fabrication is not surprising, since important factors that are likely to influence the fabrication rate vary by region.

For example, while PES interviews to identify undercount were being conducted at the end of June and into July of 1990, most of the northeast and midwest had very pleasant weather. Much of the south and west, however, had long periods with temperatures near or above 100 degrees. Denver, for example, had eleven consecutive days at the end of June and the beginning of July with temperatures of 95 degrees or higher, including five days with temperatures in the 100s. Atlanta had seventeen consecutive days with temperatures of 89 degrees or higher, followed by several days of rain.

Thus it is not surprising that fabrication seems to have been a more serious problem in these areas. Moreover, since fabrication also varies substantially by neighborhood, with interviewers being more likely to fabricate records in neighborhoods they perceive as dangerous than in safer neighborhoods, it also varies by race and by owner-renter status. It therefore appears that fabrication can account for a substantial portion of the undercount differentials identified between regions, between types of city, and between population groups.

---

11. West, *P-6 Report: Fabrication in the P-Sample.*
12. Ibid.

Ambiguity or Misreporting of Usual Residence

The question of where someone lives is often not as straightforward as it may seem. The census uses the concept of "usual" address: if you are staying somewhere temporarily and usually live somewhere else, you are instructed to report your usual address instead of your address on April 1. For many people, this instruction is ambiguous and subject to varying interpretation. "Snowbirds," who migrate between the north and south, can give the address where they spend the largest part of the year, or the address where they spend the largest part of their life, or the address where they are registered to vote, or the address where they feel most at home, or the address where they happen to be on April 1. They might give one answer when they fill out their census form in April and a different answer when they are interviewed for the coverage survey in July.

Other people who move to or from temporary quarters at about the time of the census can also claim a usual address different from the place where they were located on census day. For example, college students who are packing up to move out of a dormitory room that they will never see again may use their "home" address instead of the college address that the Census Bureau would prefer. In comparison with an estimated national undercount of only 1 percent or 2 percent of the population, these components of the population with an indistinct usual place of residence represent a very significant component of the population.

Thus the task of determining the appropriate address for each census respondent amounts to replacing the traditional concept of usual address, which is defined largely by the respondent, with a set of assignment rules developed by the designers of the coverage survey. This replacement can involve the reassignment of large numbers of people, and it can potentially have a larger effect on

53

regional population distribution than census undercount itself.

Given the large number of people with an indistinct usual place of residence, it is not surprising that the Census Bureau's Evaluation Follow-Up Study found many P-sample respondents who were classified as nonmovers for purposes of calculating the undercount adjustments, but were identified by new information as having moved in after census day. Weighted to a national level, they represented 274,000 persons,[13] or about 5 percent of the estimated national net undercount. (Of course, the effect on the individual poststrata that were most affected would have been greater.) It should be noted that these figures do not reflect the full magnitude of the problem of indistinct "usual" place of residence: they reflect only those cases—presumably a small minority—for which the PES was judged to have classified movers incorrectly.

Finally, it should be noted that different cities and different neighborhoods can vary greatly in their proportion of people with an indistinct usual place of residence. If the sample drawn for a particular poststratum happens to include some block clusters in a college town or in a retirement community, then its adjustment factor will be very strongly affected by this problem. The adjustment for a class of cities in a broad geographic area can thus be determined largely by whether or not the sample includes a few "outlier" blocks.

---

13. The P-4 report and P-16 report indicated that "census day address error" increased the undercount estimate by 811,000 persons. The Census Bureau subsequently indicated, however, that this figure included other errors found by the P-sample re-interview as well. The conclusion that 274,000 persons were found to have been added to the undercount estimate through incorrect assignment of census day address by the PES is based on subtracting these other errors, which represent 537,000 persons labeled "P-sample re-interview" in Leo Breiman's paper, from the 811,000 persons initially identified as "census day address error" in the Census Bureau reports. See Breiman, "Undercount or Bad Data?" pp. 467, 471, and 475.

Geocoding Errors

Another task that proves to be very difficult is coding addresses to the proper census block. Coding a record to the wrong census block is a very serious problem for an undertaking that depends on matching records between two surveys. If a census record that belongs in a sample block has been mistakenly coded to a different block, it may not be found. The corresponding PES record would therefore be erroneously classified as missed by the census. Conversely, if an otherwise valid census record has been mistakenly coded to the sample block, it may be counted as an erroneous enumeration when it fails to match with a PES record and when residents of the block indicate that no such person lives there. To reduce the magnitude of these problems, both PES records in the P-sample and census records in the E-sample were checked against one or two rings of surrounding blocks. According to the P-11 report, 4.08 percent of the P-sample was matched to the census through geocoding to the surrounding blocks, but only 2.29 percent of the E-sample was classified as correctly enumerated as a result of matching with PES records in surrounding blocks. If matching to surrounding blocks had not been done, this difference would have been equivalent to an approximate excess of 4,296,000 in the P-sample population.[14]

This difference highlights the sensitivity of the PES analysis to variations in methodology and procedure. As was pointed out by Leo Breiman, "The implication of this result is that, if the surrounding blocks search had not been done, then geocoding errors would have caused a doubling of the . . . national estimated undercount to over 4 percent. On the other hand, using a larger search area

---

14. Randall Parmer, *P-11 Report: Balancing Error Evaluation*, U.S. Bureau of the Census, 1990 Post-Enumeration Survey Evaluation Project, Series #M-2, attachment (1991).

might well have produced a much lower undercount estimate."[15] Since 38 percent of the households that were matched outside their proper block in the 1986 PES rehearsal were matched more than five blocks away,[16] an expanded search area might have had a very significant effect on the measure of undercount.

The sensitivity of the PES analysis to small errors is also illustrated by another geocoding problem encountered by the PES. It was found that two particular block clusters initially increased the undercount estimate by nearly 1 million people because of faulty census geocoding. Most of the people in those blocks had been counted by the census, but many of them were identified as uncounted because they had been erroneously coded as living in different blocks. It is somewhat disconcerting that only two block clusters out of a total of 5,290 included in the PES can erroneously contribute nearly 1 million people to the undercount estimate, especially since the total estimated net undercount is only about 5 million. Of course, in this case the problem was obvious enough to be identified: the influence of these block clusters was downweighted so that they contributed "only" 150,000 to the estimated undercount.[17] One has to wonder, however, how many similar problems may have gone undetected and uncorrected.

Unreliable Interviews

Another problem that the PES must contend with is unreliable interviews. Interviews can be unreliable for many

15. Breiman, "Undercount or Bad Data?" p. 468.

16. Kirk M. Wolter, "Technical Feasibility of Adjustment," memorandum to the Undercount Steering Committee, Bureau of the Census, Washington, D.C. (1987).

17. Howard Hogan, "Downweighting Outlier Small Blocks," STSD 1990 Decennial Census Memorandum Series #V-109, addressed to John Thompson, Chief, Statistical Support Division, Bureau of the Census, Washington, D.C., June 18, 1991.

reasons, including interviewer errors, language barriers, lack of information on the part of respondents (some of whom are children and some of whom are neighbors, landlords, or other nonmembers of the household), and lack of cooperation on the part of respondents (some of whom are criminals, illegal immigrants, psychotics, or practical jokers). The serious implications of this problem for measurement of undercount through a coverage survey are demonstrated in the P-9a report.

The Evaluation Follow-Up project conducted new interviews for a sample of PES E-sample records. The new interview information was given to matching teams with instructions to change match status only if new, relevant, and reliable information was present in the new interview. The result was that 13 percent of the records changed match status. In fact, a majority of these changes (7 percent of the records examined) involved changes from "erroneous enumeration" to "correct enumeration" or vice versa; the remainder (6 percent of the records examined) involved changes from one of these categories to "unresolved" or vice versa.[18] Although proponents of adjustment stress the fact that the changes had a general tendency to cancel each other out and that they had fairly little effect on the net undercount estimates, the more pertinent implication for the present analysis is that a very substantial proportion of cases from the Post-Enumeration Survey had very uncertain match status.

Whether these changes in match status are attributable to unreliable information in the initial interviews or merely to a tendency for match status to change each time a different team of matchers examines a difficult case, the fact remains that we are trying to measure a subtle phe-

---

18. Kirsten K. West, *P-9a Report: Accurate Measurement of Census Erroneous Enumerations,* U.S. Bureau of the Census, 1990 Post-Enumeration Survey Evaluation Project, Series #K-2 (1991); Eugene P. Ericksen, Stephen E. Feinberg, and Joseph B. Kadane, "Comment," *Statistical Science,* 9(4): 512 (1994).

nomenon with a very crude instrument. Based on the findings in the P-9a report, weighted to reflect the national population, more than 2 million persons would have changed from "correctly enumerated" to other classifications, and more than 1.6 million persons would have changed from "erroneously enumerated" to other classifications.[19] In the context of a net national undercount of only about 5 million people, the magnitude of these reclassifications suggests very serious problems resulting from unreliable interview data.

Unresolvable Cases

After all of the follow-up, review, and rematching involved in the 1990 PES, there were still 5,359 E-sample cases and 7,156 P-sample cases that remained unresolved and had to be imputed. This represents approximately 1.6 percent of the total combined P-sample and E-sample cases. On the one hand, the fact that the number was not larger is a testimony to the persistence and ingenuity of the PES staff. On the other hand, it must be noted that the percentage of unresolved cases was very close to the total percentage of the population that is believed to be undercounted. Thus unresolved cases are not a small problem, but rather a problem that can have a critical effect on the undercount estimate. As Breiman notes, the undercount estimate would nearly double if all the unresolved P-sample cases were assumed to be unmatched and all the E-sample cases were assumed to be correctly enumerated, but the opposite assumptions would suggest a census overcount of 1 million persons.[20]

The match status of the unresolved cases was imputed through a complex regression model that involved esti-

19. West, *P-9a Report: Accurate Measurement.*

20. Parmer, *P-11 Report: Balancing Error Evaluation*; Breiman, "Undercount or Bad Data?" p. 468.

mating coefficients for dozens of variables.[21] Regardless of the complexity of the methodology or the carefulness of its assumptions, however, it must be recognized that all the cases we are talking about here are cases that could not be classified as matches or nonmatches even after careful and repeated review of all the information available about them. Very little is known about what proportion of unresolvable survey responses really do match with one another. An imputation process may be able to produce a "reasonable" allocation of records to matched and unmatched status, but it cannot classify them definitively. A reasonable allocation would be sufficient if the proportion of unresolved cases were very small relative to the rate of undercount, but it is not sufficient when the proportion of unresolved cases is nearly as great as the net rate of undercount. The large number of unresolvable cases is by itself a fatal flaw in the undercount analysis.

Effect of Identified Sources of Error on the Undercount Adjustments

We have seen that the undercount measurements are subject to several serious sources of error. To determine whether these errors can serve as a solution to the paradox identified at the beginning of this chapter, it is necessary to see whether their combined effect would elevate the undercount estimates enough to offset the tendency for the coverage survey to miss many of the same people who are missed in the census.

Several attempts have been made to quantify the net effect of identified measurement errors on the 1990 estimates of undercount. The analysis in the Census Bureau's

---

21. T. R. Belin, G. J. Diffendal, S. Mack, D. B. Rubin, J. L. Schafer, and A. M. Zaslavsky, "Hierarchical Logistic Regression Models for Imputation of Unresolved Enumeration Status in Undercount Estimation," *Journal of the American Statistical Association*, 88:1149–66 (1993).

P-16 report indicates that corrections for measurement errors in the 1990 PES would have decreased the undercount estimate from 2.1 percent to 1.4 percent.[22] A later analysis by the same author incorporated additional corrections related to a major computer processing error discovered by the Census Bureau in late 1991, the rematching of records in some suspect blocks, and the inclusion of very late census data that had not been available when the initial PES estimates were developed. This analysis suggested that corrections for identified measurement errors would have reduced the undercount estimate from 2.1 percent to 0.9 percent.[23]

An analysis by Leo Breiman, which built on the Census Bureau analyses cited above, incorporated additional sources of error to arrive at an adjusted undercount estimate of only 0.6 percent.[24] This does not mean that the "true undercount" was only 0.6 percent, but merely that this is the amount of apparent undercount identified by the 1990 coverage survey that remains after making rough adjustments for the errors that have been identified and documented. Breiman's estimates of the effect of each error source, based on data from the Census Bureau evaluations, are shown in table 3–1. Breiman concludes that about 70 percent of the net undercount adjustment that had been proposed for the 1990 census count—3,706,000 out of 5,275,000 persons—actually reflects identified measurement errors rather than actual undercount.

Despite their differences, these three studies all point clearly to the same conclusion: there are enough measurement errors that inflate the undercount estimate to roughly offset the large number of people who appear to be missed by both surveys. This conclusion provides the

---

22. Mulry, *P-16 Report: Total Error in PES Estimates.*
23. Mary H. Mulry, "Total Error of Post-Census Review Estimates of Population," Decennial Statistical Studies Division, U.S. Bureau of the Census, Washington, D.C., July 7, 1992.
24. Breiman, "Undercount or Bad Data?" p. 475.

TABLE 3–1

EFFECT OF IDENTIFIED SOURCES OF ERROR ON THE
1990 CENSUS UNDERCOUNT ADJUSTMENTS

Error Source	Number of Persons Erroneously Added to Undercount
P-sample rematching	553,000
Census day address errors	274,000
Fabrications	50,000
E-sample rematching	624,000
E-sample re-interview	− 473,000
P-sample re-interview	537,000
Ratio estimator bias	290,000
Computer coding error	1,018,000
Late-late census data	183,000
New out-of-scopes in rematch	164,000
New out-of-scopes in re-interview	358,000
Re-interview of noninterviews	128,000
TOTAL	3,706,000
Estimate of identified net undercount prior to correction for identified errors	5,275,000
Estimate of identified net undercount after correction for identified errors	1,569,000

NOTE: Like the original PES estimates of undercount, these estimates of PES error are subject to both sampling error and nonsampling error. Moreover, it is likely that they fail to identify all the problems of the PES. Nevertheless, these estimates are more than adequate for the present purpose of demonstrating that the 1990 coverage survey involved a very large amount of measurement error and that its identified errors are sufficient to explain the paradox laid out at the beginning of this chapter. But they should not be interpreted as producing a definitive estimate of the amount of "true" undercount that was identified by the 1990 PES.

SOURCE: The first seven of these error sources are considered in the P-16 report, and the first nine error sources are considered in the subsequent Census Bureau report by the same author: Mary H. Mulry, "Total Error of Post Census Review Estimates," Decennial Statistical Studies Division, U.S. Bureau of the Census, Washington, D.C., July 7, 1992. With the exception of the count of census day address errors, these figures are taken from table 15 of Leo Breiman, "The 1991 Census Adjustment: Undercount or Bad Data?" *Statistical Science,* 9(4): 458–537 (1994). That table indicated 811,000 census day address errors, based on the P-4 and P-16 reports. As explained in note 13 above, that figure is corrected here to 274,000. This correction is also reflected in Breiman's finding that correction of identified errors would lower the undercount estimate to 0.6 percent. Excluding that correction, Breiman's adjusted undercount estimate was only 0.4 percent.

solution for the paradox identified at the beginning of this chapter.

Thus it appears that the 1990 coverage survey missed a very substantial number of people who were missed by the census, but that it also identified a large number of people as missed by the census who actually had been counted. Moreover, there is a large amount of additional error—far greater in magnitude than the level of under-count—that is less visible at the broadest level of aggregation because the errors in one direction are offset by errors in the other direction. Thus while the 1990 coverage survey suggests an overall level of undercount similar to that indicated by demographic analysis, it cannot be relied on to shed light on patterns of undercount for different demographic components of the population or for different geographic areas. The differential undercounts indicated by the coverage survey largely reflect differences in the incidence and direction of survey matching errors and other methodological problems rather than differences in the incidence of census undercount. As noted in chapter 2, these problems do not reflect deficiencies in the skill and effort applied to the task by the Census Bureau, but rather they reflect the impossibility of adequately measuring undercount in this manner.

4
Concluding Observations

Media accounts of the census sampling controversy frequently suggest that all the scientific arguments favor the Census Bureau's plans to adjust the next census for undercount. It is often implied that any opposition to the proposed approach must be based on brazen partisanship or on some sort of resistance to scientific methods.

Nevertheless, the preceding chapters demonstrate that there are compelling scientific arguments against the Census Bureau's approach. That is not to say that sampling has no place in the census. The argument is not against sampling in the abstract, but against the particular approach that has been proposed: even an otherwise valid statistical analysis tends to produce faulty results when it relies on faulty data and faulty assumptions.

The proposed approach involves a survey, taken several months after the census itself, that attempts to recount all the people in a sample of geographic areas. When this survey counts someone whose census record cannot be found, that person is generally assumed to have been missed by the census. When people who had been counted in the census fail to appear in the survey, they are investigated to find out if they really exist. The census count for each segment of the population is then adjusted up or down based on its apparent overcount or undercount in the sample areas. Although this approach appears reasonable at first glance, closer examination reveals ample evidence of faulty data and faulty assumptions.

One of the key weaknesses of this approach is that many people who do not participate in the census will not participate in the sample survey either. Many do not really want the government to know where they are: millions of people have reason to steer clear of immigration authorities, police, civil courts, and bill collectors. Others are missed because they are hard to find: homeless people are very hard to count, for example, as are people living in housing units that do not look like separate housing units. Such problems affect the survey as well as the census. Many of those who avoided the census are unlikely to step forward a few months later when their neighborhood is singled out for a special visit by another government enumerator. Some who were hard for census-takers to find will be hard for survey-takers to find as well, and the survey does not even attempt to count homeless people. In short, it is simply not accurate to assume that, within each designated segment of the population, people who were missed by the census will be just as likely to participate in the survey as those who were counted by the census.

Given the obvious inability of the survey to reach many of the people who were missed by the census, its initial results were very surprising. The adjustments that were proposed for the 1990 Census actually reflected a higher rate of apparent undercount than did the Census Bureau's more reliable "demographic analysis" method. Even after the bureau corrected some of the problems it had found, the total national undercount derived from the survey was very close to the total undercount suggested by demographic analysis. How can a post-census survey produce such results if it misses many of the people who were missed by the census?

The explanation for this paradox is that people can be falsely identified as "missed" by the census when an error is made in matching their survey response with their census response. The Census Bureau usually figures out which person is which, but it has to deal with clerical errors, language barriers, aliases, wrong information from neighbors of people who are not at home, people who move after the census, people who pull the interviewer's leg, interviewers who make up data on hot or rainy days, and a host of other problems. Such problems make it impossible to achieve perfect accuracy in matching the survey to the census. And virtually perfect accuracy is required to make the adjustment method work: with only a small percentage of the population missed by the census, even a tiny rate of error in classifying the rest of the population can overwhelm the actual undercount.

That is exactly what happened in 1990. The Census Bureau's evaluation studies uncovered serious problems with matching error, fabrication of interviews, ambiguity or misreporting of usual residence, geocoding errors, unreliable interviews, unresolvable cases, and other problems. When the bureau summarized these findings, it found that about 57 percent of the apparent net undercount actually represented bias caused by various errors in measuring undercount. Subsequent analysis outside the bureau suggests that the figure was at least 70 percent. Thus many of the people who would have been added to the 1990 population count had not really been missed by the census: the adjustment process would have caused them to be double-counted. Meanwhile, many of the people who really were missed by the census were missed by the survey too, since they were just as hard to find or just as unwilling to participate as they had been for the census. These problems cannot be corrected by trying a little harder, or by increasing the sample size, or by making minor improvements in the methodology: they are inherent flaws of any attempt to measure undercount by matching the individuals found by a coverage survey with the individuals found by the census.

These problems explain why the measurements of undercount did not follow a consistent pattern, and why the adjustments derived from them were inconsistent with the pattern of undercount revealed by demographic analysis. The errors in measuring undercount—sometimes very large errors—varied greatly from one place to another and from one demographic category to another, and the pattern of errors will vary from one census to another as well. This means that all comparisons based on census data will come into question if the proposed adjustment method is used. Some of the large differences between one segment of the population and another or between one time period and another will be caused by errors in the adjustment factors, but no one will know which differences are valid and which are not. We expect a census to increase our knowledge about how our communities are changing and how they compare with other communities, but a census that incorporates faulty adjustments for undercount would increase our ignorance instead.

These arguments may seem surprising to people whose familiarity with this issue is limited to claims reported in the news media that all the good arguments favor the Census Bureau's approach. It should be remembered, however, that statisticians and demographers raised strong arguments against that approach at the beginning of this decade. In fact, it was their position that eventually prevailed when the secretary of commerce concluded that the proposed method was too unreliable to use for adjusting the 1990 Census. Their arguments at the beginning of the decade could not be refuted, and—if the appendixes of this volume are any indication—there are many strong arguments against the bureau's approach that cannot be refuted at the end of the decade either.

APPENDIX A

Responses to Questions from the Honorable Carolyn B. Maloney on Census Undercount Adjustment

Following are twenty-five questions submitted by the Honorable Carolyn B. Maloney on May 13, 1998, and the responses by the author of this monograph.

This appendix reflects minor stylistic editing of the questions and answers that appear in the official records of the House Subcommittee on the Census, and references have been modified to reflect the structure and pagination of this volume.

QUESTION 1
Can you tell us about a statistical or scientific activity that you've worked on that either worked perfectly the first time you tried it, or that didn't work as well as you had hoped the first time so you abandoned the idea altogether without making an effort to improve or redesign it?

RESPONSE
Very early in my career, I had an experience with this dilemma which I believe can shed a great deal of light on the process of computing adjustments for census undercount.

In the first government agency I worked for, I was once asked to do a quick analysis to show the cost of excess hospital capacity in Michigan. I had a pretty good idea what to expect based on the published literature on the subject, but my first calculations showed just the opposite of what I expected.

Naturally, the question I asked myself was, "What did I do wrong?" When I reviewed my computer program with this question in mind, I found a simple computational error that explained a large part of the problem. The figures still did not point in the expected direction, but at least they did not point so strongly in the "wrong" direction.

I could not find any more mistakes in my program, so the next question I asked myself was, "How can I improve the analysis?" Since I had been taking a very simple approach to a very complex question, it did not take long to find that I had left out some important factors which biased the results in the "wrong" direction. When I repeated the calculations with allowances for those factors, I got the results that I expected.

Unquestionably, the changes I made were improvements. I had produced an analysis that was consistent with my expectations about what was true and with the published literature on the subject. But that experience left me with two important questions.

First, What would have happened if my initial results had been consistent with my expectations? Would I even have found my computational error if I had not had to ask myself, What did I do wrong?

Second, What would have happened if my expectations and the initial results had been the opposite of what actually happened? What if I had expected excess hospital capacity to *decrease* hospital expenditures instead of increasing them, and what if my first calculations had shown an increase? Would I have been able to find some legitimate factors that were left out of the initial analysis which biased the results in this new direction? Would I have "improved" the analysis in the opposite direction if I had the opposite expectations?

I had encountered a dilemma that faces all researchers, whether they are aware of it or not. On the one hand, it is probably impossible to produce good research on a complicated problem without finding and correcting mistakes and modifying methods based on new insights that are gained in the course of the analysis. And a principal way to find those mistakes and gain those new insights is by finding things that are contrary to expectations and figuring out either what went wrong or how the data and the analysis can be improved.

On the other hand, when the corrections and refinements are driven by expectations of what the results should be, the research will tend to conform to those expectations regardless of whether those expectations are correct and regardless of whether the data and methodology are sound.

I believe that this personal experience and this dilemma shed much light on the process of measuring undercount through a post-enumeration survey. In one respect, the analysis of the Post-Enumeration Survey is exactly the opposite of the analysis described above: instead of being too simple, it is incredibly complex. Yet it illustrates the dilemma of expectation-driven analysis even better than my personal experience: matching survey responses with census responses is so difficult and it involves so many errors of so many types that it sets up an impossible dilemma for the Census Bureau. On the one hand, it is necessary to monitor the quality of processes to ensure that they are producing plausible results, to check outliers and disparities, to look for problems, and to correct problems when they are found. On the other hand, those necessary measures tend to make the results conform to expectations, irrespective of the correctness of the expec-

69

tations or the soundness of the underlying data and methodology.

Some of the corrections that were made had a very large effect on the final adjustments for undercount. For example, when certain blocks seemed to have too much undercount, records were sent for rematching and they came back with different results: rematching just 104 out of 5,290 block clusters resulted in a decrease of 250,000 in the estimated net national undercount. When other blocks had obvious problems attributable to geocoding errors, they were "downweighted" so they would have less effect: downweighting just two block clusters reduced their effect on the national net undercount from nearly 1 million persons to only about 150,000 persons. A computer programming error was found that contributed more than 1 million persons to the net national undercount. Without these three corrections, the final estimate of net undercount would have been about 40 percent higher than it was, and it would not have been plausible even at the broadest national level. On the one hand, it would be difficult to argue that these corrections should not have been made. On the other hand, it is clear that there were enough remaining errors that any of the adjustment factors could still have been "corrected" significantly in either direction.[1]

One of the paradoxes of the PES analysis is that it produced a seemingly plausible picture of undercount at the broadest national level despite its many obvious flaws. Once the potential role of expectations in refining the data is understood, however, this is not surprising at all. Given enough time, resources, and methodological flexibility, the adjustment factors could probably be corrected

---

1. Most of the errors listed in chapter 3 of this volume have not been corrected, even in the Census Bureau's latest set of undercount adjustments for 1990. A notable exception is the computer coding error. Sources of error are also listed in chapter 2 of this volume, and further evidence of high error levels is presented in chapter 3.

until they produced virtually any pattern of undercount that is deemed plausible.

QUESTION 2

Despite the fact that the Census Bureau made improving the count among minorities a major goal of the 1990 Census, the 4.4 percent differential in the 1990 undercount between blacks and non-blacks was the highest ever recorded. Experts have repeatedly said that spending more money on traditional methods will not reduce this differential. If not through statistics, how do you propose to reduce this differential?

RESPONSE

First, I would like to comment on the observation that the differential undercount in 1990 was the highest ever recorded. It is true that the difference between the estimated undercount for blacks and the estimated undercount for other races increased from 4.3 percentage points in 1970 to 4.4 percentage points in 1990.[2] It would be a mistake, however, to suppose that the undercount has been getting worse in each census. In fact, according to the Census Bureau's "demographic analysis" method, the undercount for blacks in 1990 was the second lowest ever recorded. Likewise, the 1990 undercount for whites was the second lowest ever recorded, and the overall undercount was the second lowest ever recorded. The lowest undercounts ever recorded were in 1980.

Thus, the two most recent censuses have been our most accurate in history with respect to undercount. Although there is certainly room for improvement, it is evident that the Census Bureau's efforts to improve the count have met with considerable success. The widespread discouragement and negativism with regard to so-

---

2. A table showing the estimated undercount rates for each census since 1940 appears in chapter 2 of this volume. Changes in undercount rates over time are also addressed in the answer to Question 5 below.

called traditional methods is unwarranted.

My suggestions for reducing undercount and reducing the undercount differential fall into two general categories: first, improving the census enumeration, and second, *estimating* the amount of undercount for those demographic groups and levels of geography for which reliable estimates can be made instead of *adjusting* for undercount.

Improving the Census Enumeration. Most of the following suggestions for improving the count are not original, and they can be considered "traditional methods," like those that have made the last two censuses the most successful in our history:

• The master address file (MAF) is a key to the success of the census. The local review program and other efforts to improve the MAF should receive all the resources and attention that they need to succeed.

• Another key to the success of the census is the number and quality of enumerators. One reason for the success of the 1980 Census may have been the large number of recent college graduates who were unemployed and available to work for the Census Bureau. With the aging of the baby boom generation, such a pool of labor was not available for the 1990 Census. Because of a relatively small number of young people and the possibility of a continued sound economy, recruitment of skilled temporary workers for Census 2000 may be very difficult. Meeting this challenge needs to be a high priority.

• Yet another key to the success of the census is adequate time in which to conduct follow-up. If Integrated Coverage Measurement is not implemented, some of the time currently allotted to the coverage survey could be used for regular census operations.

• Since many households have more than five members, the standard census form should have room for information on more than five people.

• An effort should be made to ensure that every household receives all the census forms that it needs *before* census day. The proposed use of pre-census reminder cards is a promising innovation. The bureau could consider the possibility of including return-cards that households can use to request foreign-language forms, extra forms for additional household members, and any other special forms and assistance that the household might need.

• Some households include members who may want to keep their census information confidential from other members of the household (or from whom the rest of the household may want to keep their census information confidential). There could be provisions for them to receive and submit separate census forms.

• The traditional "substitution" process for non-respondents and partial respondents could be modified so that the mixture of respondents in the "deck" from which substitutions are made reflects the characteristics of nonrespondents and partial respondents, rather than reflecting the characteristics of the population as a whole. This should reduce the undercount differential.

Many other good ideas for improving the enumeration have been suggested by other analysts, and many have already been adopted by the Census Bureau.

Estimating Undercount Instead of Adjusting for Undercount. Even after every effort to achieve the best possible count, some segments of the population will not have been fully counted. This problem can be addressed more appropriately through *estimates* of undercount than through *adjustments* for undercount. The advantages of approaching undercount in this manner include the following:

• An estimate of undercount would not have to be released until it is completed and evaluated. An adjustment

73

for undercount would have to be finalized very quickly to meet the statutory deadlines for completion of the census.

• An estimate of undercount could be revised as more is learned about patterns of undercount in the census. An adjustment for undercount could not be changed even after it is found to be faulty, since it would be the official census count and since it would be reflected in hundreds of census products that would not be feasible to replace.

• An estimate of undercount could use all relevant sources of valid information. The proposed method of adjusting for undercount is limited to one source of information—a post-enumeration survey—which misses many of the same people who are missed by the census and identifies many people as missed by the census who were not missed at all.

• An estimate of undercount could be developed for only those levels of geography for which it is reliable. For example, if a methodology works well at the state and national levels but not at the local level, undercount estimates would not have to be made at the local level. In contrast, the proposed adjustment for undercount would be applied all the way down to the block level.[3]

QUESTION 3
You have mentioned your concerns about block level accuracy. Can you discuss your thoughts on the accuracy of census numbers at the state level if Dual System Estimation is used in 2000? Do you have any evidence that suggests that the census counts will be more accurate at the state level in 2000 if DSE is not used?

RESPONSE
The central flaws of the proposed method of adjusting for undercount are, first, that it misses many of the same people who are missed by the census, and second, that

---

3. The advantages of approaching undercount through population estimates instead of through census adjustments are discussed further in response to Question 8 below.

many—in fact, most—of the people that it identifies as missed by the census were not missed at all.[4] Thus, any differences it suggests between states are not so much differences in the amount of undercount as they are differences in the amount of error that the Census Bureau makes in trying to measure undercount.

Several of the sources of bias noted in my testimony are of particular relevance at the state level. For example:

- The exclusion of homeless people from the Post-Enumeration Survey results in a bias against states whose homeless people are more likely to be staying with households during the April census than during the subsequent post-enumeration survey.

- Differences in weather and climate can affect the level of fabrication in the post-enumeration survey, which in turn can have a very serious effect on the apparent undercount rate.[5]

- Because differences in weather and climate influence the likelihood that people will be at home when an enumerator visits, they can affect the proportion of successful PES interviews in different states. A high rate of unsuccessful interviews or proxy interviews in the PES can seriously increase the level of error in measuring undercount.

- When people migrate from one state to another on a seasonal basis, the post-enumeration survey can assign them to a different state from the one they reported as their "usual" state of residence when they filled out their census form.[6]

QUESTION 4
Secretary Mosbacher, in testimony before both the House and the Senate, said that the Post-Enumeration Survey

---

4. See chapters 2 and 3 of this volume.

5. The apparent effect of weather on the rate of fabrication is discussed in chapter 3 of this volume.

6. The accuracy of adjusted population counts at the state level is discussed further in response to Questions 4 and 20 below.

would make the majority of the states more accurate. Is that statement correct? If so, why is his testimony so at odds with your testimony?

RESPONSE

In the Notice of Final Decision regarding adjustment of the 1990 Census, Secretary Mosbacher wrote:

> Based on the measurements so far completed, the Census Bureau estimated that the proportional share of about 29 states would be made more accurate and about 21 states would be made less accurate by adjustment. . . . When the Census Bureau made allowances for plausible estimates of factors not yet measured, these comparisons shifted toward favoring the accuracy of the census enumeration. Using this test, 28 or 29 states were estimated to be made less accurate if the adjustment were to be used. . . . While we know that some will fare better and some will fare worse under an adjustment, we do not really know how much better or how much worse. If the scientists cannot agree on these issues, how can we expect the losing cities and states as well as the American public to accept this change?[7]

This statement by Secretary Mosbacher is not at odds with my testimony. The figures cited, which involve comparing the adjusted counts to calculations based on assumptions about actual undercount in each state, are consistent with everything I have said about high levels of error in the Post-Enumeration Survey. An adjustment methodology that seemed to be less accurate than the census for twenty-one or twenty-eight or twenty-nine states in

---

7. U.S. Department of Commerce, Office of the Secretary, "Adjustment of the 1990 Census for Overcounts and Undercounts of Population and Housing; Notice of Final Decision," *Federal Register*, July 22, 1991, p. 33583.

1990 can hardly be considered a sound basis for fine-tuning the results of the next census.[8]

QUESTION 5
The 1990 Census cost 20 percent more per household in real dollars than the 1980 Census. The 1980 Census cost twice as much per household in real dollars as the 1970 Census. That is an increase in real dollar cost per household of 250 percent with no improvement in the differential undercount. Does that suggest to you that spending more on traditional methods will reduce the differential undercount?

RESPONSE
In addressing this question, it is important to remember that the 1980 and 1990 censuses were the most successful in history with respect to minimizing undercount. Based on the Census Bureau's demographic analysis method, the 1.8 percent estimated undercount in 1990 compares favorably with the estimated undercounts for 1940 (5.4 percent) through 1970 (2.7 percent). Likewise, the estimated undercount for blacks in 1990 (5.7 percent) compares favorably with the estimated undercounts for blacks for 1940 (8.4 percent) through 1970 (6.5 percent). The estimated 1990 undercounts for blacks, for other races, and for the population as a whole are the second best ever recorded; the only census with better results was the 1980 Census.[9]

My assessment of these figures is that the Census Bureau has made a lot of progress through the so-called

---

8. The accuracy of adjusted population counts at the state level is discussed further in response to Question 3 above and Question 20 below.

9. A table showing the estimated undercount rates for each census since 1940 appears in chapter 2 of this volume, and progress in reducing differential undercounts is discussed in the first part of the response to Question 2 above.

traditional methods. Since a number of promising improvements have been incorporated in the plans for Census 2000 and further improvements remain to be explored, it appears that the traditional methods hold promise for further progress.[10]

QUESTION 6

Demographic analysis showed higher undercounts of African Americans than the undercounts demonstrated by the Post-Enumeration Survey. That suggests that the Post-Enumeration Survey understates, not overstates, the undercount, especially for minorities. In other words, isn't it likely that the 1990 Census missed more African Americans than would have been added back into the census by the Post-Enumeration Survey?

RESPONSE

As you note, there are substantial discrepancies between the undercounts suggested by the Post-Enumeration Survey and those suggested by demographic analysis. These discrepancies can be seen in table 2–2 of this volume: relative to the results of demographic analysis, the undercount adjustments that were proposed for the 1990 census were 36 percent too low for black males but 43 percent too high for black females at the national level. The adjustments for other males were about right at the national level, but the adjustments for other females were 133 percent too high. Subsequent to correction of several errors, the adjustments proposed in September 1992 were 42 percent too low for black males and 33 percent too high for black females at the national level. The adjustments for other males were 25 percent too low, and the adjustments for other females were 50 percent too high. The situation was even worse at the regional level, where the proposed

10. Some of the options for improving the census count are discussed in the response to Question 2 above.

adjustments presented an inconsistent mosaic of high and low adjustments for different age, race, and sex categories.

The birth data and other data used in demographic analysis provide a very solid basis for estimating the relative number of males and females that were missed by the census. The discrepancies between the PES and demographic analysis therefore demonstrate quite clearly that the undercount adjustments derived from the PES are implausible and unreliable. One obviously cannot go beyond that, however, to characterize them as consistently overstating or understating the undercount of minorities.

QUESTION 7

You have talked a lot about bias in the Post-Enumeration Survey but have not talked much about the bias in the census. The differential undercount measured by demographic analysis shows that bias in the census is quite real. If there is no Integrated Coverage Measurement, is it not the case that this bias in the census will continue?

RESPONSE

The various techniques for conducting a more accurate enumeration—including those listed in my response to Question 2 above, those discussed in reports by the National Academy of Sciences, those proposed by the Census Bureau, and others as well—can be expected to promote a modest improvement in undercount rates. As explained in my response to Question 2 above, I believe that the remaining undercount is best addressed through population estimates rather than through census adjustments.

QUESTION 8

Do you believe that it is acceptable for the census to consistently miss certain segments of the population—African Americans, Latinos, Asian Americans, poor people in rural and urban communities—at greater rates than the white population? If that is not acceptable, what do you

propose be done to reduce the differential undercount? Can you offer any evidence that your proposal(s) will reduce the differential undercount?

RESPONSE

Although the Census Bureau tries very hard to count everybody and makes special efforts to count minorities and persons in poor communities, there are still some people who are missed. Regardless of whether they are missed because their living arrangements make them hard to count or because they intentionally avoid the census, it is desirable to know how many people each community really has and what their characteristics are.

But the methodology that has been proposed for adjusting the census is not acceptable: it reflects survey matching error more than it reflects undercount, it would greatly reduce the value of subnational census data, it would invalidate comparisons over time, and it would not be demographically credible even at the national level.

I do not know of any methodology that can produce acceptable adjustments for undercount. Such a methodology would have to meet several difficult criteria. Some of the criteria that come to mind are:

• It would have to reflect undercount, and not some other phenomenon that is distributed differently from undercount.

• It would have to be simple enough to be completed and verified within the tight statutory time frame for producing the census count.

• It would have to be sound enough to be recognized as valid and to need no major corrections or revisions after the census count is published.

• The level of sampling error and other errors would need to be small enough that they would not affect analysis of local census data more seriously than undercount itself.

• Variations in error over time would need to be small

enough that they would not invalidate comparisons of detailed census data over time.

The proposed adjustment methodology does not meet any of these criteria, and I know of no alternative adjustment methodology that meets them all. As indicated in the answer to Question 2 above, the problem of undercount can be addressed by conducting a more complete count, and developing *estimates* of undercount instead of *adjustments* for undercount. A properly designed estimate could meet the first and last criteria, and the remaining criteria would be inapplicable or relaxed. An estimate would be subject to review and revision, it would not have to be subject to a tight statutory time frame, and it would not have to be applied to small units of geography unless it were found to be valid for small units of geography.

QUESTION 9
It has been stated that one of the faults of the 1990 PES was correlation bias. Can you explain correlation bias? I understand that it is the likelihood that the people missed in the census may be the same people missed in the PES. Said another way, both the census and the survey miss the same people, for example, young black males. How does correlation bias affect the accuracy count of those traditionally undercounted, blacks, Hispanics, Native Americans, renters?

RESPONSE
Your understanding of correlation bias is correct. Correlation bias should lead to a very substantial underestimate of the undercount for those groups that tend to be missed by both surveys.

QUESTION 10
Wouldn't the only risk of correlation bias be minimization of the undercount rather than overestimation of the undercount?

RESPONSE

That is only one of the risks. Another problem is that some communities might have more correlation bias than others. This is one of several factors that can cause the adjusted counts to be less indicative of a community's share of the nation's population than the original counts.

Another problem with correlation bias is that analysts who dismiss it as innocuous sometimes seem to forget that it is there. Correlation bias should result in adjustments for undercount that are much too low. The undercount adjustments derived from the 1990 Post-Enumeration Survey, however, were *not* much too low: they were much too high for some segments of the population, much too low for others, and about on target for the national population as a whole. Analysts who forget about correlation bias and focus only on the seemingly plausible picture of undercount for the national population as a whole can make the mistake of thinking that the PES provides reasonably accurate information about undercount. For analysts who do *not* forget about correlation bias, however, the fact that the adjustments derived from the PES are not consistently too low is a clear sign that there is something seriously wrong with them.

QUESTION 11

In testimony before the Senate Committee on Governmental Affairs approximately one year ago, Dr. Lawrence Brown, Professor of Statistics at the University of Pennsylvania, stated that "Statistical sampling methods can be used in an effective and objective way to assist the census process." Do you agree with Dr. Brown's statement? If you disagree, please explain why.

RESPONSE

While I do not disagree with this statement, I would add that statistical sampling methods can be used in ways that are effective and ways that are ineffective, in ways that are objective and ways that are biased, and in ways that assist and ways that detract from the census process. Like any tools, statistical sampling methods work better for some purposes than for others, and they can be used in both appropriate and inappropriate ways.

QUESTION 12
Dr. Lawrence Brown also testified before Senator Thompson that the Sampling for Non-Response Follow-up plan "is an objective procedure all the way around and has a very good chance of working as desired." Do you agree with that statement? If you disagree, please explain why.

RESPONSE
My testimony and analysis have focused exclusively on the issue of undercount adjustment, and I have not comprehensively reviewed the methodology proposed for handling non-response. Nevertheless, the following observations should be helpful for understanding some of its shortcomings.

An underlying premise of sampling for non-response is that each census statistic will be based mostly on actual responses, and that it will therefore not be seriously affected by minor errors in estimating the characteristics of the remaining 10 percent or so of the population from a sample.

One critical statistic for which this premise does not hold is the vacancy rate. Obviously, most vacant households will not respond to the census. It is my understanding that most of them are to be excluded from follow-up based on reports by letter carriers that they are vacant. (The plan calls for a sample of these housing units to be followed up, however, in order to adjust for inaccuracies in the letter carriers' vacancy reports.) Any vacant units that the letter carriers do not report as vacant are to be followed up on a sample basis along with other non-responding households.

Unfortunately, neither the letter carrier reports nor the proposed samples will produce reliable vacancy data. The letter carrier reports tend to be inaccurate, their errors cannot be corrected very well through the proposed sample, and the routine sampling of non-responding housing units will be subject to error as well.

In its preliminary testing, the Census Bureau found that 42 percent of the housing units that letter carriers identified as vacant were actually occupied, and that half the units pre-identified as vacant were not identified as such by the letter carriers. If this result is at all indicative of the level of error to be expected in the letter carrier reports, they provide a very poor basis for determining vacancy status.

These deficiencies of the letter carrier reports cannot be corrected adequately even through the 30 percent sample recently proposed. Variations in the accuracy of letter carrier reports from neighborhood to neighborhood and from carrier to carrier will present a serious dilemma: if the correction factors are derived from broad geographic areas, they will not be applicable to neighborhoods where vacancy status is particularly easy or particularly hard to determine, nor to neighborhoods where the letter carrier has particularly high or particularly low levels of skill and conscientiousness in determining vacancy status. But if they are derived from small geographic areas, they will tend to be dominated by sampling error. Whichever way the Census Bureau chooses to resolve this dilemma, the correction factors will be unreliable for small units of geography. The poor overall quality of the letter carrier reports, in turn, will cause those unreliable correction factors to have a very large effect on the vacancy rates.

A similar dilemma arises in connection with vacant units in the regular sample of non-responding households. The number of vacant units missed by the letter carriers can be expected to vary widely from neighborhood to neighborhood: data derived from broad geographic areas will therefore not be indicative of local conditions, but data derived from small geographic areas will tend to be dominated by sampling error. Finding even one vacant housing unit in the sample can cause several housing units to be considered vacant, which can substantially change the vacancy picture for a census block or a small community. Any error—whether sampling error or non-sampling error—will therefore tend to have a serious effect. And since we are talking about measuring a (usually) small proportion of households through a small sample drawn from a small population, relatively high levels of error can be expected.

These problems would be much less serious if 90 percent of the data on vacancy were based on actual enumerations and only 10 percent of the data were subject to substantial error. That will not be the case, however, because of the fact that most vacant housing units do not respond to the census. Unlike most other census statistics, the numerator of the vacancy rate is to be *almost entirely* based on very imprecise data.

A problem with faulty vacancy rates is far more critical than it may seem at first glance. In addition to being an important statistic in its own right, the vacancy rate plays a crucial role in determining the census count itself. If the estimated vacancy rate for a unit of government is 2 percentage points too low, then people will be imputed as living in vacant housing units and we can expect the population count to be a little more than 2 percentage points too high. If the estimated vacancy rate is 2 percentage points too high, then housing units that are occupied will be assumed to be vacant and we can expect the population count to be a little more than 2 percentage points too low.

Errors of this magnitude and greater would be quite likely for many units of government, particularly where there is a substantial amount of seasonal or vacation housing. For example, 49 percent of the units of government

85

in Michigan had vacancy rates of 10 percent or more in 1990, 31 percent had vacancy rates of 25 percent or more, and 14 percent had vacancy rates of 50 percent or more. The proportion of housing units in these areas whose vacancy status would be determined by very imprecise methods would therefore be quite substantial, and the resulting census counts could easily be off by *several percentage points.*

As a demographer involved in the production of intercensal population estimates, I am very much aware of the weaknesses and limitations of those estimates and of the need for periodically benchmarking them to new census counts. I am therefore alarmed by the prospect that the proposed methodology might produce census counts for many units of government that are less reliable than their intercensal population estimates based on the 1990 Census, and that future population estimates for these areas might have no accurate basis at all.

Another potential problem with sampling for non-response is the possibility of distortions in local population data caused by replicating cases encountered in the sample. For example, if the methodology turns one household with a grandmother caring for grandchildren into several local households with grandmothers caring for grandchildren, or one household with twelve children into several local households with twelve children apiece, then the local census data will be seriously distorted. Thus, it would not be appropriate to replicate the findings from the sample within a small geographic area. (It may be appropriate, however, to use large-area samples as a basis for assigning weights to local census responses to influence the composition of the deck used for imputing the characteristics of non-responding households.)[11]

---

11. This option is discussed further in the response to Question 2 above. An additional problem with sampling for non-response—high error rates in the data recorded for people who refuse to be interviewed or who are never found at home by the interviewer—is discussed in the response to Question 24c below.

QUESTION 13

In addition, Dr. Brown testified that the Census Bureau's 2000 Census plan had been "drastically simplified and improved. . . . [These changes] make it possible to now believe that the Integrated Coverage Measurement might work as well as desired to correct the undercount." Do you agree with that statement? If you disagree, please explain why.

RESPONSE

I strongly disagree with this statement. The two papers that I submitted as testimony to the subcommittee on May 5, 1998, are entirely directed toward explaining my position on this question.[12]

QUESTION 14

With regard to concerns that the Integrated Coverage Measurement process could be manipulated to achieve a particular outcome in terms of the population counts, Dr. Brown testified that "if all of this planning is done in advance, it is very, very hard for me to see how one could direct these subjective decisions towards any desired goal." Do you agree with Dr. Brown that if the procedures and protocols for the Integrated Coverage Measurement are set forth in advance and subject to expert and public scrutiny, then it is very unlikely that the sampling and statistical estimation process will be subject to manipulation, possibly for political advantage? If you disagree, please explain why.

RESPONSE

Subjective decisions can bias the results in ways that are not necessarily even intentional, conscious, or politically motivated. The most frequent and most likely way for this to happen is for personnel at various levels of the ICM effort—particularly interviewers, matchers, and the man-

---

12. See chapters 2 and 3 of this volume.

agers and statisticians responsible for implementing the methodology—to be influenced in their subjective decisions by their expectations about undercount. For example, when the match status of a particular record is not clear, it is possible for the classification to be influenced by whether the matcher expects people in that demographic category to have a high level of undercount. When a PES interviewer fabricates data on a hot or rainy day for people who never seem to be at home, the characteristics assigned to those people will naturally reflect the expectations of that interviewer. When a decision is made about whether to send a group of records back for re-matching or to downweight a group of records as outliers, that decision can be influenced by whether the initial findings for those records were consistent with expectations about undercount and by whether the overall level of apparent undercount is higher or lower than expected.

QUESTION 15
Dr. Brown also testified that even after the non-response follow-up phase of the census is complete, there "would still [be] the undercount problem of those people who just refuse to be counted or are very difficult to count." Do you agree with that statement? If you disagree, please explain why.

RESPONSE
I agree with that statement. A substantial portion of this problem is already handled through the Census Bureau's traditional "imputation" or "substitution" process for non-respondents and partial respondents. The importance of this element of the census process is frequently overlooked and, as explained in the answers to Questions 2 and 12, this process can be improved. The remainder of the problem, as explained in the answers to Questions 2 and 8, can be better solved through an *estimate* of undercount rather than an *adjustment* for undercount.

QUESTION 16

With regard to the Post-Enumeration Survey in the 1990 Census, Dr. Brown testified that many of the difficulties with the procedure "can be traced to the fact that the PES sample was much too small to support the kind of objective, reliable analyses that are desired." Do you agree with that? If you disagree, please explain why.

RESPONSE

One of the interesting things about measuring undercount through a post-enumeration survey is that the process has several fatal flaws, any one of which is sufficient by itself to explain why it produces such unacceptable results. One such flaw is sampling error attributable to a sample size that was insufficient to support the detailed stratification that the undercount adjustments require. This was such a big problem that there is no implausible aspect of the 1990 adjustments for which it is not a plausible explanation.

It would be a fallacy, however, to conclude that sampling error is therefore the only explanation or even the chief explanation for the many implausible aspects of the 1990 adjustment factors. There are several other documented problems that are also sufficient by themselves to explain them. For example, the documented level of uncertainty and error in matching is sufficient to explain any of these implausible results.[13] The level of fabrication in typical surveys, which was generally confirmed by the various studies of fabrication in the PES, is comparable in size to undercount and is sufficient to explain any of these implausible results.[14] Likewise, any of the implausible results can be explained by the fact that such an attempt to measure a small component of the population is ex-

---

13. Uncertainty and error in matching are discussed in chapter 3 of this volume.

14. The problem of fabrication is discussed in chapter 3 of this volume.

tremely sensitive to tiny errors in the insurmountable task of classifying the remainder of the population.[15] It would be foolish to presume that solving only one of these problems would be sufficient to "fix" the proposed process for measuring undercount. There would be more than enough problems remaining to invalidate the results.

QUESTION 17
The size of the sample in the Integrated Coverage Management is 750,000 households. Is that a proper size for such an endeavor?

RESPONSE
It is more than sufficient for the Post-Enumeration Survey's traditional role of evaluating census questions and procedures. No increase in sample size, however, would be sufficient to produce valid adjustments for undercount through a post-enumeration survey, since sample size is not the only problem or even the chief problem. As explained in the answer to Question 16 above and in the papers that I submitted to the subcommittee as testimony on May 5, 1998, the attempt to measure undercount through a post-enumeration survey has several fatal flaws that are not caused by insufficient sample size. These flaws account for much of the estimated undercount and, since they involve non-sampling error, they obviously will not be reduced by enlarging the sample. In fact, an increased sample size, coupled with a very tight time schedule and questionable staffing levels, is likely to increase the problems of fabrication, proxy interviews, and matching error that plagued the 1990 PES.

QUESTION 18
The results of the PES in 1990 showed that census was less accurate than its predecessor. That result was con-

---

15. The sensitivity of the adjustments to small errors is discussed in chapter 2 of this volume.

firmed by demographic analysis, which has been performed on every census since 1940. We certainly know that the 1990 Census was much more expensive than the 1980 Census. Do you agree with the conclusion that 1990 was also less accurate than 1980?

RESPONSE

I have not studied this issue in detail. As explained in the answer to Questions 2 and 5 above, however, it is appropriate to say that the Census Bureau's demographic analysis method indicated that the 1980 Census was the most accurate in history and that the 1990 Census was only the second most accurate in history with respect to net undercount.

QUESTION 19

Please explain the difference between net over- or undercount in the 1990 census count and actual over- and undercounts (mistakes) made in the 1990 count. I know that a net undercount of 1.6 percent sounds relatively small but for census purposes, aren't those 26 million mistakes a concern?

RESPONSE

There are three sets of terms that need to be explained: *actual* gross overcount and undercount, gross *measured* overcount and undercount, and net measured overcount and undercount.

Actual gross overcount is the number of people *actually* counted twice by the census or counted in error. For example, people who were born after April 1 or who died before April 1 are sometimes counted by the census even though they should not be. College students who are counted at their parents' home instead of at the school where they lived are considered part of the "overcount" of their parents' community and part of the "undercount" of their college community. Overcount is usually referred to as "erroneous enumeration." Similarly, "actual gross undercount" is the number of people *actually* missed by the census.

Gross measured overcount and gross measured undercount are appropriate terms for the number of people identified as erroneous enumerations by the Post-Enumeration Survey and the number of people identified as undercounted by the Post-Enumeration Survey. The "26 million mistakes" to which the question refers represent gross measured overcount and gross measured undercount. These numbers are much higher than *actual* gross overcount and *actual* gross undercount for several reasons:

- Much of the measured undercount and overcount is attributable to measurement errors in the Post-Enumeration Survey rather than actual undercount and overcount in the census. This is the central point developed in this volume.

- All the people who are added to the census count through the substitution process and all the people whose census responses are too incomplete to be used for matching are considered to be erroneous enumerations. The corresponding people who are found in those housing units by the Post-Enumeration Survey are considered to be part of the gross undercount. While this is appropriate in the context of the PES analysis, it does tend to make the gross measured overcount and gross measured undercount misleadingly high.

- People who seem to be counted in the wrong location by the census are counted as part of the undercount in one place and part of the overcount in another. This is appropriate in the context of the PES analysis, but it tends to make the total number of errors appear misleadingly high.

- Matching errors in the PES analysis typically involve a census record that should be matched with a PES record but that fails to match for any one of a number of reasons.

In most such cases, the census record becomes part of the gross measured overcount and the PES record becomes part of the gross measured undercount. Again, this is appropriate in the context of the overall PES analysis, but it does tend to make the gross measured overcount and gross measured undercount misleadingly high.

(It should be noted that matching error does not always result in offsetting errors in gross overcount and gross undercount. For example, when people described by the unmatched census records really do exist, it can be difficult to prove that they do not exist and they might therefore not become part of the measured overcount. This is one of the ways that matching error introduces bias into the undercount adjustments.)

• Looking at the PES in a broader sense, it can be expected that the number of people erroneously identified as overcounted or undercounted will naturally tend to exceed the number of people erroneously identified as counted correctly. This is because only a very small proportion of the population is actually overcounted or undercounted: in other words, there are very few people at risk of being *erroneously* identified as counted correctly. The vast majority of people are counted correctly by the census, however, and they are therefore at risk of being erroneously identified as overcounted or undercounted. This results in a large upward bias in the gross measured overcount and the gross measured undercount.

Net measured undercount can be simply computed by subtracting gross measured overcount from gross measured undercount. (If an area has more measured overcount than measured undercount, its net measured overcount can be calculated by subtracting its net measured undercount from its net measured overcount.)

Thus, the frequently cited figure of 26 million mistakes is greatly inflated, and it does not reflect the actual level of accuracy in the 1990 Census.

QUESTION 20

I understand that improvement in the average does not necessarily mean that there will be improvement in every case. In 1990, there was criticism about the strata being broken down by region. If statistical methods are used in 2000, with strata broken down by state in 2000, can we expect more states with improved accuracy than there were in 1990?

RESPONSE

Since the undercount adjustments reflect error in measuring undercount more than they reflect undercount itself, any prediction of how the numbers will fall out in any particular census is very uncertain. With that caveat, my expectations are as follows:

* Estimating the adjustments for each state individually will negate most of the advantage otherwise gained from a larger sample size in terms of sampling error.
* The factors that introduced geographic bias into the 1990 undercount adjustments will tend to affect individual states in the same way that they affected regions in 1990.[16]
* Since state boundaries are as artificial as regional boundaries in terms of having a logical relationship with undercount rates, I see no reason at this time to expect an increase in accuracy resulting from this change in stratification.[17]

QUESTION 21

Representative Sawyer pointed out that the longer the Census Bureau is in the field, the higher the error rate in the information collected. I believe that information came

---

16. Some of the factors contributing to geographic bias are described in the response to Question 3 above.

17. The accuracy of adjusted population counts at the state level is also discussed in response to Questions 3 and 4 above.

from one of the many GAO studies he and his Republican colleagues commissioned. You have stated your concern about the Census Bureau not being in the field for enough days in the 2000 plan. Can you explain the difference in opinion?

RESPONSE

There is no contradiction between the findings that you cite and the concern about trying to process more interviews with inadequate staff in a shorter period of time. In fact, the findings reinforce the concern.

The higher error rates during the final weeks of follow-up do not result simply from "being in the field too long." The first weeks in the field result in more accurate data because they involve actual interviews with people who are willing to be counted. The final weeks in the field result in less accurate data because they involve more interviews with people who have resisted repeated attempts to count them, more proxy interviews to "close out" cases for which a direct interview cannot be obtained, and more fabrication of interviews in response to pressure to close out as many cases as possible before the deadline.

Shortening the amount of time in the field does not eliminate those final weeks of interviewing in which high error rates can be expected. The final weeks of interviewing will still be there, with all of their pressure to close out the difficult cases. Instead of eliminating the *final* weeks of interviewing, the current plan would, in effect, eliminate the *initial* weeks of interviewing in which lower error rates can be expected. By calling for more PES interviews in a shorter period of time with inadequate staff, the current plan creates a danger that the initial weeks of interviewing will be as error-prone as the final weeks of interviewing were in 1990.

It should be noted that the accuracy problems in the final weeks of interviewing and the concerns about truncated time frames apply both to the census itself and to the post-enumeration survey. Proxy interviews, fabrication by interviewers, and unreliable reports by respondents are problems for the PES as well as for the census—in fact, they are even more serious when they occur in the PES. The timetable for Census 2000 involves very tight time frames for both the census and the PES.[18]

QUESTION 22

In order to address the problem of declining public response, the GAO suggested exploring a radically streamlined questionnaire in future censuses. Would you give us your thoughts on how effective this approach might be in increasing response, and also its effect on perhaps diminishing the usefulness of census data?

RESPONSE

I have not studied this question in detail. I understand that the Census Bureau has concluded from its research that shortening the form would not have a large effect on response rates. I do know, based on the involvement of my office in the Census Bureau's survey of data users and from its work in disseminating census data and in using census data to address needs of data users, that the information on both the long form and the short form is very widely used in both the public and private sectors. A radically shortened questionnaire would greatly diminish the value of the census. *If* we have a successful census in 2000, however, and *if* the Continuous Measurement program is adequately funded and successfully implemented, it should be possible to eliminate the long form in 2010.

QUESTION 23

In its 1992 capping report on the 1990 Census, the GAO concluded that "the results and experiences of the 1990 census demonstrate that the American public has grown

---

18. High error rates in the data collected by the sample surveys are discussed further in response to Questions 24(a) and 24(c) below.

too diverse and dynamic to be accurately counted solely by the traditional 'headcount' approach and that fundamental changes must be implemented for a successful census in 2000." Do you agree with that conclusion? If you disagree, please explain why.

RESPONSE

It is not entirely fair to criticize a statement removed from its context within a larger report, so the following comments should not be interpreted as a criticism of the GAO or its 1992 report.

• First, it is important to realize that our diverse and dynamic population is not a new development. Our history has included settlement of the frontier, Indian wars, emancipation of slaves, massive foreign immigration, industrialization, urbanization, the Great Depression, suburbanization, interstate redistribution of population, and many other events and changes that have always made our population diverse, dynamic, and challenging to count. As difficult as it is to develop a precise Master Address File for Detroit in 1998, it would have been far more difficult in 1898.

• Second, I agree with the notion that there is considerable room for improvement in the census and that census methods should adapt to changes in the population. I am not exactly sure, however, what is meant by "fundamental" changes. The concept of finding out how many people there are by counting them is sound, and I would characterize the required improvements as incremental rather than fundamental.

• Third, the deficiencies of the census require not simply "change" but rather "change for the better." It should be clear from my testimony and the testimony of the other members of the May 5, 1998, panel that the particular uses of sampling that have been proposed for Census 2000 would be very serious changes for the worse.

• Fourth, the 1990 Census approached our "diverse

97

and dynamic" society, in which it is often difficult to find people at home, through a mail-back census form with instructions available in thirty-four different languages. It is somewhat ironic that the innovation proposed for dealing with these problems is a post-enumeration survey that relies exclusively on *personal interviews* by enumerators, most of whom speak fewer than thirty-four languages. The proposed innovation is more poorly adapted to our diverse and mobile society than the census itself.

QUESTION 24(a)
After the 1990 census, GAO concluded that "the amount of error in the census increases precipitously as time and effort are extended to count the last few percentages of the population. . . . This increase in the rate of error shows that extended reliance on field follow-up activities represents a losing trade-off between augmenting the count and adding more errors." In the last months of the follow-up efforts in 1990, GAO estimated that the error rates approached 30 percent, and that this problem was probably exacerbated by the use of close-out procedures. This appears to be a problem inherent to the methodology of the 1990 Census. Don't you agree?

RESPONSE
It is inherent not just to the census, but to any survey that must obtain information about people who are difficult to reach or resistant to being counted. These problems apply even more to Sampling for Non-Response and to the post-enumeration survey required for Integrated Coverage Measurement than they do the census itself. Not only do these efforts involve exhaustive follow-up of difficult cases, but any errors will be multiplied when the sample results are inflated to represent the sampled universe. In fact, given the proposed constraints of time and resources discussed under Question 21 above, the proposed plans for Census 2000 can be expected to make these problems

even worse. Again, it must be stressed that we need not just "change," but "change for the better." The proposed changes are even more susceptible to this problem than the old procedure was.[19]

QUESTION 24(b)
Do you have any information on the error rates for information gathered using close-out procedures?

RESPONSE
The Census Bureau would be the most authoritative source for such information.

QUESTION 24(c)
Even if sampling is not perfect, isn't its error rate well below the levels for the last percentages of the population using more traditional follow-up procedures?

RESPONSE
The premise underlying this question appears to be that sampling is somehow an *alternative* to traditional follow-up procedures. But traditional follow-up procedures are just as much a part of the proposed uses of sampling as they are of the conventional census: follow-up is a critical part of Integrated Coverage Measurement, and follow-up is what Sampling for Non-Response is all about. Both these efforts involve exhaustive efforts to obtain information about that last percentage of the population, and the associated errors will be compounded when the sample findings are inflated to represent the sampled universe. The pertinent comparisons would therefore be between the overall error of the traditional census and the overall error of the modified census, or else between the error resulting from close-out procedures for the samples and

---

19. High error rates in the data collected by the sample surveys are discussed further in response to Question 21 above and Question 24(c) below.

the error resulting from close-out procedures for a traditional census. It should be obvious from the discussion above that these comparisons would not be favorable to the proposed sampling methodology.

That having been said, we are still left with a question about the overall error rate for sampling. With regard to sampling for undercount, a Census Bureau report estimated that identified errors accounted for about 33 percent of the net undercount suggested by the 1990 PES. A subsequent analysis by the same author raised this estimate to about 57 percent, and a further analysis by Leo Breiman raised the estimate to about 70 percent.[20] Similarly, another Census Bureau report stated that "about 45 percent of the revised estimated undercount is actually measured bias and not measured undercount. In seven of the ten evaluation strata, 50 percent or more of the estimated undercount is bias."[21] These error rates compare unfavorably with error rates for virtually any aspect of the census process, regardless of whether or not such comparisons can be pertinently drawn.

QUESTION 24(d)
If this is the case, then doesn't that logically lead to GAO's and the Commerce Department's inspector general's conclusion that sampling at least a portion of the nonresponding households would increase the accuracy and decrease the cost of conducting the census?

RESPONSE
Even if the sampling methodologies did not share the census's reliance on error-prone efforts to resolve difficult cases, the issues raised in the response to Question 12

---

20. These reports are discussed in chapter 3 of this volume.
21. Department of Commerce, Bureau of the Census, "Assessment of Accuracy of Adjusted versus Unadjusted 1990 Census Base for Use in Intercensal Estimates: Report of the Committee on Adjustment of Postcensal Estimates" (the CAPE Report), August 7, 1992.

above would still be pertinent. While there may be a place for sampling in improving the census, the particular procedure proposed for sampling nonrespondents appears to have some serious shortcomings.

QUESTION 25

GAO also concluded after the 1990 Census that a high level of public cooperation is key to obtaining an accurate census at reasonable cost. Unfortunately, the mail response rate has fallen with every census since 1970, and was only approximately 65 percent in 1990. The reasons for this decline are in many instances outside of the Census Bureau's control, for example, the increase in commercial mail and telephone solicitations and in nontraditional household arrangements. For these reasons, the Bureau is planning a public education campaign for the 2000 Census, surpassing any previous attempts. Given the response in 1990, do you believe this is money well spent?

Do you believe that this public education campaign can succeed in arresting the decline in response rates?

Even if it does, wouldn't some use of sampling be warranted to solve the problems associated with reaching the last few percentages of nonresponding households?

RESPONSE

Taking the last question first, some of the appropriate and inappropriate uses of sampling with respect to non-response are addressed in the answer to Question 12 above.

I agree that a high level of public cooperation and a high response rate are keys both to obtaining an accurate census and to holding down costs. While I have not reviewed the Census Bureau's publicity plans, I understand that they involve improvements to both the quality and the timing of the publicity efforts. (See also the answers to Question 2 and Question 5 above regarding the success of "traditional methods" in improving census participation.)

It should be noted that the issue of undercount adjustment also has very significant implications for levels of public cooperation and response.

On the one hand, there is reason to believe that a decision to adjust the census would have a very serious negative effect on census participation. If people expect the census count to be adjusted, they may not think that the effort required to complete their census form is necessary. Similarly, the critical involvement of public officials and temporary census employees in securing high participation rates might be jeopardized by a decision to adjust the census. In the Notice of Final Decision on adjustment of the 1990 Census, then-Secretary of Commerce Robert Mosbacher wrote:

> I am worried that an adjustment would remove the incentive of states and localities to join in the effort to get a full and complete count. The Census Bureau relies heavily on the active support of state and local leaders to encourage census participation in their communities. . . . If civic leaders and local officials believe that an adjustment will rectify the failures in the census, they will be hard pressed to justify putting census outreach programs above the many other needs clamoring for their limited resources. Without the partnership of states and cities in creating public awareness and a sense of involvement in the census, the result is likely to be a further decline in participation. . . .[22]

> There is a real risk that, with an expectation of a correction through adjustment, the field staff would not have the same sense of commitment and public mission in future censuses and, as a

22. Department of Commerce, Office of the Secretary, "Adjustment of the 1990 Census for Overcounts and Undercounts of Population and Housing; Notice of Final Decision," *Federal Register,* July 22, 1991, p. 33584.

result, careless and incomplete work would increase, thereby decreasing the quality of census
data. These are the workers the Bureau depends
on to collect the data from the groups that are
hardest to enumerate. If these data suffer, the
information lost at the margin is information
that is especially important to policy development.[23]

On the other hand, the current controversy over adjustment may play a positive role in encouraging census
participation. This controversy has increased awareness of
the importance of being included in the census on the
part of civic leaders, local government officials, civil rights
organizations, and the general public. It might be possible
to translate this awareness into something that everybody
will find superior to an adjustment for undercount: a census in which people get counted the first time.

---

23. Ibid., p. 33605.

APPENDIX B

A Debate on Adjusting the Census for Undercount

This appendix consists of three documents that are not part of the published record of the Subcommittee of the Census. The first document is a letter from the Honorable Carolyn B. Maloney, ranking minority member of the Subcommittee, to James F. Holmes, acting director of the Census Bureau. This letter served to initiate the debate. The second document is a memorandum addressed to the Subcommittee by Preston J. Waite, an assistant director of the Census Bureau. The final document is a rejoinder to that memorandum by the author of this monograph.

The appendix reflects minor stylistic editing of the rejoinder that was submitted to the House Subcommittee on the Census.

Letter from the Honorable Carolyn B. Maloney, Ranking Minority Member of the Subcommittee on the Census, to James F. Holmes, Acting Director of the Bureau of the Census, May 14, 1998

At a hearing of the Government Reform and Oversight Subcommittee on the Census on May 5, 1998, Mr. Kenneth Darga from the Office of the State Demographer, Michigan Department of Management and Budget, submitted two papers for the record. These papers are highly critical of the methods and results of the Post-Enumeration Study (PES) conducted following the 1990 Census. I am writing to request that the Census Department officially respond to Mr. Darga's work so that too can be included in the hearing record.

Mr. Darga submitted two papers, *Straining Out Gnats and Swallowing Camels: The Perils of Adjusting for Census Undercount* and *Quantifying Measurement Error and Bias in the 1990 Undercount Estimates.* In the first paper, the author contends that "although the results of [the PES] appeared plausible, at least at the broadest national aggregation, the method cannot produce reliable adjustments for undercount: It is not capable of counting many of the people who are missed by the Census, it is very sensitive even to extremely small sources of error, and it is subject to many sources of error that are very serious." The differences between the PES and the original Census data, in the author's opinion, may represent the difficulties in matching records between two surveys, rather than a true net undercount.

The author further contends that it is thus "not surprising to find that many of the detailed undercount measurements for 1990 were implausible and, in some cases demonstrably false. In an effort to correct a net national undercount of less than 2 percent, spurious undercounts of 10 percent, 20 percent and even 30 percent were identified for some segments of the population." Here the author seems to be referring to certain selected undercount adjustments for children under age ten from the 1990 PES.

Mr. Darga concludes that using the adjustments of the PES in 1990 "would have had a devastating impact on the usefulness and accuracy of Census data at the state and local level," and that "similar problems can be expected . . . for Census 2000: The problems are not due to minor flaws in methodology or implementation, but rather to the impossibility of measuring undercount through the sort of coverage survey that has been pro- posed."

Mr. Darga's second paper purports to identify and

quantify several specific types of error, including survey matching error, fabrication of interviews, ambiguity or misreporting of usual residence, geocoding errors, unreliable interviews, and unresolvable cases. His analysis draws heavily on twenty-two unpublished reports, issued in July 1991 under the title "1990 Post-Enumeration Survey Evaluation Project" by the Census Bureau, and upon the work of Dr. Leo Breiman, an emeritus professor of statistics at the University of California, Berkeley. The quantified results of the errors identified by the author lead him to conclude that "about 70 percent of the net undercount adjustment that had been proposed for the 1990 Census count—3,706,000 out of 5,275,000 persons—actually reflects identified measurement errors rather than actual undercount."

The author infers from these data that the 1990 PES "missed a very substantial number of people who were missed by the Census, but that it also identified a large number of people as missed by the Census who actually had been counted." His overall conclusion is that while the results of the PES and demographic analysis are very similar, the PES "cannot be relied upon to shed light on patterns of undercount for different demographic components of the population or for different geographic areas."

As I am sure you agree, Mr. Darga's conclusions about the reliability of the 1990 PES should not go unanswered for our hearing record, even if they represent only a small minority of scientific opinion on the issue. Please address all of the author's criticisms, including ones I may not have mentioned. Please provide your reply by May 29, 1998. Thank you for your attention to this matter.

Memorandum for the Record: The Census Bureau's Response to Papers Submitted to the House Subcommittee on the Census on May 5, 1998

The following was submitted by Preston J. Waite, assistant to the associate director for decennial census, U.S. Bureau of the Census.

This memorandum addresses concerns raised by Mr. Kenneth Darga in the two papers, "Straining Out Gnats and Swallowing Camels: The Perils of Adjusting for Census Undercount" and "Quantifying Measurement Error and Bias in the 1990 Undercount Estimates," submitted for the record at the May 5, 1998, hearing of the Government Reform and Oversight Subcommittee on the Census. Both papers are critical of the methods and results of the 1990 Post Enumeration Survey (PES).

In the papers, Mr. Darga asserts that "although the results of the 1990 PES appeared plausible, at least at the broadest national aggregation," it is not an acceptable method for census adjustment because it: (1) is incapable of counting people missed in the census and (2) is subject to serious errors. Further, Mr. Darga contends that the undercount rates produced from the survey are spurious for certain segments of the population and, therefore, would decrease the accuracy of local population counts. It is his belief that observed differences between the PES and the census data represent difficulties in matching census records to PES records, rather than an actual undercount in the census. In the end, Mr. Darga states that it is impossible to measure undercount "through the sort of coverage survey that has been proposed."

The issues raised by Mr. Darga are not new to the undercount/adjustment debate. Powerful arguments about coverage measurement have been made in support of adjustment of the decennial census as well as against adjustment. There is a growing body of literature documenting both positions in this controversy. Mr. Darga has chosen the strategy of challenging the quality of the coverage survey that provides the data used to produce the undercount rates. In the paragraphs that follow, we will attempt to address some of the statements made by Mr. Darga. The Census Bureau has a strong commitment to producing high-quality, accurate, impartial census numbers, and this commitment extends to the coverage survey data and the coverage improvement methodology.

The PES Is Not Capable of Counting Many of the People Who Are Missed by the Census. The claimed inability of the PES to count people who are missed by the census appears to be based on the premise that most people who are omitted from the census are "homeless" or "people who do not want to be counted." The argument focuses on "drug dealers, fugitives, and illegal immigrants [who] were afraid to fill out the census form that everyone [sic] in the nation received." This seems to imply that the American people can be divided neatly into two groups: those who are nearly impossible to count and those who are trivially easy to count. In fact, the census-taking situation is more complex. Mr. Darga's discussion focuses heavily on correlation bias but fails to mention the inherent differences between the census enumeration process and the survey methodology. People may be missed for many reasons: (1) if their housing unit is not included on the Census Bureau's address list; (2) if their housing unit is listed, but the post office delivers the questionnaire to the wrong address, or the census taker goes to the wrong address; (3) if they move close to Census Day; (4) if they misunderstand the questionnaire; or (5) if the census taker fails to ask the questions correctly. The list of examples is endless.

There are indeed people who are actively hiding from the government and who are nearly impossible to count. However, it would not be true to say that all illegal immigrants are hiding from the government and are missed by the census. The same argument pertains to "drug dealers" and "fugitives." Thus, the very premise on which the statement is based does not hold. We do not believe people can be divided into two groups, one group with a near zero chance of being counted and another with a near certain chance of being counted. Rather there are many different groups with many different chances. Clearly, most people fall into the near certain group, which is why the census is, on average, so complete, but also why the PES is capable of counting many of the people who are missed by the census.

Mr. Darga acknowledges that overall demographic analysis results are very similar to the undercount rates based on the PES data. As a general observation, we note that we expect to find differences between different approaches. Based on our knowledge of their strength and weaknesses, we find the agreement between the results produced by the demographic analysis and the Dual System Estimation (DSE) undercount rates based on the PES to be reassuring. We would go so far as to argue that the agreement between the 1990 PES and demographic analysis on the undercount rate is more than a happy coincidence; it is remarkable and strengthens our belief about the overall credibility of the results.

The PES Is Subject to Errors. Mr. Darga examines different error sources in the PES and reaches the conclusion that 70 percent of the net undercount adjustment reflects measurement error rather than actual undercount. The Census Bureau readily acknowledges that there are sampling and nonsampling errors in the PES. In fact, in 1991 and 1992, an extensive evaluation program of the PES estimates was implemented. These evaluations addressed the potential sources of nonsampling error in the PES that could bias the results, including matching error and errors in determining erroneous enumerations. The results of these studies were combined to produce an estimate of the overall bias in the net undercount rate at the U.S. level and thirteen high-level geographic areas. It was the finding that at the U.S. level, when correlation bias is taken into account, about 22 percent of the revised estimate of undercount (1.6 percent) was bias and not measured undercount. This is substantially less than the figure claimed by Mr. Darga. Even if the effect of correlation bias is ignored, our estimate of bias is well below the 70 percent referenced by Mr. Darga. It also should be noted that while Mr. Darga spends considerable time discussing non-sampling errors via short illustrations, no mention is made of what we actually know about the effects of these errors.

The Undercount Rates for Certain Segments of the Population Are Spurious. Mr. Darga contends that "many of the detailed undercount measurements for 1990 were implausible and, in some cases demonstrably false." He states that "in an effort to correct a net national undercount of less than 2 percent, spurious undercounts of 10, 20 and even 30 percent were identified for some segments of the population." Here, the reference appears to be to certain selected undercount rates for children under age ten from the 1990 PES. This example is misleading. The undercounts of 10, 20 and 30 percent are rare exceptions, and did not occur for major segments of the population. In fact, in subsequent analyses, we find that only 2 poststrata in the final set of 357 PES poststrata were over 20 percent, 10 were from 15 to 20 percent, and 17 were 10 to 15 percent. In short, 328 of the 357 poststrata were less than 10 percent—not grounds for devastating impacts.

Furthermore, it is unclear whether Mr. Darga's calculations for children under age ten are based on the "smoothed" estimates that were intended for use in Census adjustment or on the "raw" estimates that were not so intended. The sample sizes for some of these poststrata were quite small, and the resulting variance of the raw estimates was quite large. Regardless, Mr. Darga does not discuss the role of bias and variance and the ensuing consequences. Selecting the "correct" set of factors involves consideration of both bias and variance, and that is why a detailed evaluation of the original factors was done. Given what we now know about the small sample sizes and high variances of the estimates for children under ten, Mr. Darga's use of age data to speculate about demographic trends of Asians or black homeowners is very misleading and inappropriate.

The PES Cannot Be Used to Measure Undercount. We obviously do not agree with Mr. Darga's statement ". . . similar problems can be expected . . . for Census 2000: The problems are not due to minor flaws in methodology or implementation, but rather to the impossibility of measuring undercount through the sort of coverage survey that has been proposed." With the statement, Mr. Darga appears to dismiss any adjustment methodology based on data from a coverage survey. We recognize that this is a convenient argument for Mr. Darga and one that allows him categorically to dismiss the PES.

We do not share Mr. Darga's view that measuring the undercount with a coverage survey is impossible, though we do concede it is a challenging task. Furthermore, Mr. Darga fails to acknowledge years of research and development since the 1990 Census. The statement deliberately ignores the progress that has been made in our understanding of ways to improve data collection and data processing. Technological innovations to facilitate quality control and improve coverage have been adopted for implementation in the 2000 Census. Throughout the decade, we have continued to enhance our knowledge about the causes of undercount and census coverage errors in general. Of course, the lessons learned and the progress made are of little relevance to Mr. Darga's position, but that does not undo the reality of their existence. The Census Bureau is committed to continue its quest to overcome "minor methodological flaws and implementation errors" to ensure the high quality of its data products.

Further, Mr. Darga is so determined to focus on the coverage survey itself that he fails to acknowledge the strengths of the DSE methodology that makes use of the data. The focus is strictly on data collection and the subsequent matching operation associated with the PES. No attempt is made to fully describe all the steps involved in the PES, nor to explain the DSE methodology and the statistical model of capture-recapture. Had Mr. Darga focused on the DSE methodology rather than the coverage measurement survey itself, he would probably not have stated "that based on what was provided by the Census Bureau in 1990, one could be tempted to draw the conclusion that a coverage survey can provide an incredibly accurate measure of census undercount." The PES does not directly provide the undercount rate. It provides the data to be used for developing adjustment factors based on the DSE methodology. The record should also reflect that the PES data were deemed of sufficient high quality to do so on the basis of evaluation criteria that were accepted and agreed upon prior to the 1990 Census. Given the facts, Mr. Darga has no valid basis to conclude that adjustments based on the PES in 1990 "would have had a devastating impact on the usefulness and accuracy of census data at the state and local level."

Conclusion. The arguments and the viewpoints presented by Mr. Darga are not new to the adjustment debate and have entered into many adjustment deliberations. Mr. Darga is a state demographer. We believe his contribution may lie in pointing out the value of building consistency and demographic validity checks into the evaluation of results. Mr. Darga has demonstrated how sex ratios can be a powerful evaluation tool. The Census Bureau welcomes constructive ideas on how to improve the census and how to judge its plausibility. It is important for demographers to enter the discussion and debate on the best way to produce a census that meets both statistical and demographic standards, but the message has to be fair.

Rejoinder to the Census Bureau's Memorandum for the Record Regarding Papers on Census Undercount Adjustment

The following was submitted by Kenneth Darga, senior demographer, Office of the State Demographer, Michigan Information

Center, Michigan Department of Management and Budget, on August 28, 1998.

This rejoinder assesses the Census Bureau's official response to two papers that I submitted as testimony to the House Subcommittee on the Census on May 5, 1998. That response was written at the request of the Honorable Carolyn B. Maloney, the ranking minority member of the Subcommittee, who asked the bureau to respond to all of the arguments in those papers.

The first section of this rejoinder addresses the bureau's response to each of the major arguments in the two papers. The second section addresses several additional counterarguments that are advanced by the bureau.

Status of Major Arguments

The central thesis of my two papers is that a "coverage survey" or "post-enumeration survey" cannot provide a reliable basis for adjusting the census for undercount because (a) a coverage survey misses many of the same people that are missed by the census, and (b) many of the people it identifies as "missed" by the census really have not been missed at all. Thus, the adjustments for undercount derived from a coverage survey are largely based upon the pattern of errors in measuring undercount rather than upon the pattern of undercount itself. Needless to say, the errors in measuring undercount are not necessarily distributed in the same way as undercount, which causes serious errors in the adjusted population counts. In the course of establishing this thesis, the following principal points are made:

Demographic Analysis. *As the best available measure of undercount at the national level, the Census Bureau's "demographic analysis" method provides reasonably good information about census undercount.*

Status: Not directly addressed, although the Census
Bureau's Memorandum for the Record implicitly
accepts the validity of the findings of demographic
analysis.

This point is not central to my argument, but it is
significant nonetheless because it makes my thesis much
easier to prove and much more difficult to dispute. It also
establishes the basis for the argument below in the section
labeled "Inconsistency with Demographic Analysis."

The net national undercount suggested by the 1990
Post-Enumeration Survey (2.1 percent initially, and 1.6
percent after revision) is quite close to the net national
undercount suggested by demographic analysis (1.8 percent). Proponents of adjustment like to point out the
closeness of these figures. As the Census Bureau's memorandum puts it:

> [W]e find the agreement between the results
> produced by the demographic analysis and the
> Dual System Estimation (DSE) undercount rates
> based on the PES to be reassuring. We would go
> so far as to argue that the agreement between
> the 1990 PES and demographic analysis on the
> undercount rate is more than a happy coinci-
> dence; it is remarkable and strengthens our be-
> lief about the overall credibility of the results.

Of course, this "remarkable" agreement between the
two methods is equally consistent with the thesis that the
Post-Enumeration Survey (PES) misses many of the people who were really missed by the census and that it identifies other people as "missed" when they really were not.
In fact, this agreement makes it much easier to prove that
thesis to be true: if it can be established that the PES really
does miss many of the same people, then it follows that
the only plausible way the PES can get so close to the
"right" level of undercount is by identifying a similar
number of people as "missed" when they really have not

been missed at all. Likewise, if it can be established that many of the people that the PES identifies as "missed" really were not missed, then it follows that the most plausible way the PES can get so close to the "right" level of undercount is by missing a similar number of the people who were really missed by the census. Thus, establishing either half of the thesis establishes the other half of the thesis as well.

It should be noted that my papers provide very strong arguments for both parts of the thesis, and that each part of the thesis is established independently of the other and independent of any assertions of the validity of demographic analysis. The purpose of the preceding paragraph is to show that the Census Bureau (and other readers of my papers) cannot let one part of the thesis stand without accepting the other part as well (unless, of course, they are willing to deny the findings of the Bureau's "demographic analysis" method after they have already been cited as "remarkable" support for the credibility of their results).

Correlation Bias (Missing the Same People Missed by the Census). *A post-enumeration survey is not capable of counting many of the people who are missed by the census. In particular:*

(a) *A coverage survey cannot measure the undercount of homeless people, and the PES therefore does not even attempt to address this portion of the undercount.*

(b) *The number of people who do not want to be counted is very substantial, and many of them can be expected to avoid the PES as well as the census.*

Status: Discussed but not refuted.

The Census Bureau's memorandum addresses this argument by distorting it and then asserting that its distortions are not valid:

1. The memorandum overstates my argument by asserting that:

> The claimed inability of the PES to count people who are missed by the census appears to be based on the premise that *most* of the people who are omitted from the census are "homeless" or "people who do not want to be counted" [emphasis added].

While that premise may well be true, my paper neither makes nor depends upon that premise. The argument actually made in my paper is that *many* of the people missed by the census fall into these categories.

2. The memorandum further states that the emphasis on people who do not want to be counted:

> ... seems to imply that the American people can be divided neatly into two groups: those who are nearly impossible to count and those who are trivially easy to count.

The memorandum goes on to describe various reasons for being missed by the census that cause people to fall between these two extremes, and then asserts:

> We do not believe people can be divided into two groups, one group with a near zero chance of being counted and another with a near certain chance of being counted. Rather there are many different groups with many different chances.

The problem with this argument is that there is actually nothing in my papers that suggests that the population "can be divided neatly into two groups." This notion is entirely an invention of the Bureau's Memorandum for the Record. In fact, the second paragraph of my paper clearly states:

> A major reason for the undercount—*although not by any means the only reason*—is that quite a few people do not want their identities known by the government.

Of course there are other reasons why people are missed by the census. And since those reasons often cause some of the same people to be missed by the post-enumeration survey, they bolster my argument that a coverage survey misses *many* of the same people who are missed by the census.

3. The memorandum states that:

> There are indeed people who are actively hiding from the government and who are nearly impossible to count. However, it would not be true to say that *all* illegal immigrants are hiding from the government and are missed by the census. The same argument pertains to "drug dealers" and "fugitives." Thus, the very premise on which the statement is based does not hold [emphasis added].

Of course that would not be true—that is why my paper never says it. In fact, my paper points out that the net undercount of 5 million persons is remarkably low given the facts that the United States has more than 1 million people who do not make any of their required payments on court ordered child support, 5 million illegal immigrants, and over 14 million arrests each year for non-traffic offenses. Obviously, a substantial number of these people are counted by the census—either they respond to the census themselves, someone else responds on their behalf, or they are added to the census count through the imputation process for non-respondents and partial respondents. The argument that "the very premise on which the statement is based does not hold" is totally impertinent, since both the premise and the statement are merely inventions of the Bureau's Memorandum for the Record.

Extreme Sensitivity to Small Classification Errors. *A very simple and very basic statistical phenomenon causes the under-*

count adjustments to be extremely sensitive even to very small errors in classifying people as "missed by the census" or "erroneously enumerated."

Status: Not addressed.

This is one of several arguments in my paper that is sufficient by itself to totally invalidate the attempt to measure undercount through a coverage survey.

Sources of Classification Error. *The attempt to measure undercount through a coverage survey is subject to many very serious sources of error.*

Status: Not addressed.

This argument complements the preceding argument: because the adjustments are so sensitive to errors in classifying people as "missed by the census" or "erroneously enumerated," these sources of error have a devastating impact on the accuracy of the adjustments.

Classification Errors Are Reflected in the Adjustments. *Because the coverage survey misses many of the people missed by the census and identifies other people as missed by the census when they really were not missed, the differential undercounts it suggests will largely reflect differences in the amount of error in measuring undercount rather than differences in the amount of undercount itself.*

Status: Not addressed.

Inconsistency with Demographic Analysis. *The final adjustments based on the 1990 PES are quite different from the estimates based on the Census Bureau's "demographic analysis" method even for very broad population groups at the national level.*

Status: The Memorandum for the Record asserts the opposite, but without presenting evidence or refuting the contrary evidence in my papers.

The memorandum states:

> Mr. Darga acknowledges that overall demo-
> graphic analysis results are very similar to the un-
> dercount rates based on PES data. As a general
> observation, we note that we expect to find dif-
> ferences between different approaches. . . . [W]e
> find the agreement between the results pro-
> duced by the demographic analysis and the Dual
> System Estimation (DSE) undercount rates
> based on the PES to be reassuring.

It should be noted that I acknowledge a similarity to the
findings from demographic analysis *only for the overall total
population figure.* The similarity breaks down very seriously
as soon as one starts to examine the results in any detail.
Thus, my paper states that:

> [T]he final national PES results for 1990 are ac-
> tually quite different from the estimates based
> on demographic analysis even for very broad
> population groups. The apparent undercount
> for black males is 42 percent less than the rate
> suggested by demographic analysis, and the rate
> for white, Native American, and Asian/Pacific fe-
> males is 50 percent higher.

It is hard to imagine what reassurance the Census Bureau
finds in these discrepancies.

Spurious Undercount Differentials. *Some of the large undercount differentials suggested by the 1990 Post-Enumeration Survey are definitively shown to be spurious.*
*(a)   The eighteen large differential undercounts between girls
        and boys displayed in figure 3 are implausible and they fol-
        low no discernible pattern.*
*(b)   Because of the stability of the sex ratio in this age range,
        these differential undercounts can be tested definitively.*
*(c)   These differentials are clearly spurious. The areas in ques-
        tion show no sign of differential undercount between boys*

and girls prior to adjustment. After adjustment based on the PES, the sex ratio in these areas is dramatically different from the norm.

(d.) The problems revealed here pertain just as much to other age groups as to children and just as much to other demographic characteristics as to the sex ratio. Because these undercount differentials are clearly spurious, we cannot trust a coverage survey to tell us which segments of the population have higher undercounts than others.

Status: Not refuted.

Although the Census Bureau's response does not address any of the elements of this argument listed above, it does raise two related issues:

1. The bureau's memorandum claims:

> [I]t is unclear whether Mr. Darga's calculations for children under age ten are based on the "smoothed" estimates that were intended for use in Census adjustment or on the "raw" estimates that were not so intended.

Because of conflicting information that I had received, this point was indeed unclear in the preliminary drafts of my papers that I sent to the Census Bureau for review between July 1997 and April 1998. This point was not clarified until the end of April, and the clarification is reflected in the paper submitted to the Subcommittee on the Census that the Bureau was asked to address. It is clearly stated there that these are the initial adjustment factors, prior to the application of a statistical smoothing procedure. It is further explained that these non-smoothed factors are pertinent for the current analysis, since they reflect the amount of apparent undercount actually identified by the PES. These non-smoothed factors are also the ones most relevant in the context of Census 2000, since the Census Bureau does not plan to use a statistical smoothing process in the adjustment of the next census.[1]

2. The bureau's memorandum claims:

The sample sizes for some of these poststrata were quite small, and the resulting variance of

---

1. The smoothing process that was used for the 1990 undercount adjustments was criticized for several shortcomings, including: (a) its radical departures from the original undercount measurements lacked firm support in the data, (b) alternative smoothing procedures produced very different results, (c) it did not correct the bias and other non-sampling errors that invalidate the adjustments, and (d) the adjustments were still implausible even after smoothing.

Although the bureau has decided not to use the technique that it calls "smoothing," it now plans to smooth the adjustment factors from the Census 2000 "dress rehearsal" with a mathematical technique called "raking." The bureau has not yet decided whether raking will be used in Census 2000 itself. Unfortunately, despite the change in terminology, it appears that the new technique will be subject to most of the same objections as the old one. Once again, radical departures from the undercount measurements will be necessary. (Small modifications would not be adequate to conceal the huge inaccuracies in the measurements of undercount derived from a coverage survey.) Once again, there will be many alternative ways to make those modifications that produce very different results. (The list of possible ways to transform the undercount measurements will include all the ways that were considered for 1990 and all the ways that the bureau is considering for 2000, not to mention any other ways in which the undercount estimates could be mathematically transformed to make them appear more reasonable.) Once again, the proposed technique does not address the documented biases in the undercount measurements. (The bureau attributes the shortcomings of the undercount measurements to sampling error, despite the fact that it has documented high levels of bias and non-sampling error.) And once again, implausible results can be anticipated. (Although the implausibility of the new method's results cannot be demonstrated until those results are produced, it should be noted that there is a trade-off between (a) and (d) above: maintaining any level of consistency with the results of the coverage survey will impede the correction of its implausible findings; plausible results can be produced only at the price of contradicting the pattern of apparent undercounts measured by the coverage survey.) The bureau's plans for "raking" are described in a paper by Preston J. Waite

121

the raw estimates was quite large. Regardless, Mr. Darga does not discuss the role of bias and variance and the ensuing consequences. Selecting the "correct" set of factors involves consideration of both bias and variance, and that is why a detailed evaluation of the original factors was done.

If the Census Bureau is aware of any consequences of bias and high variance that are favorable to their proposed methodology, I invite them to explain how they mitigate the arguments presented in my papers.

I agree that the sample sizes for most poststrata—that is, for most designated components of the population—were quite small, and that there were very serious problems with sampling error (that is, the variance of both the raw estimates and the final estimates was very large). It would be a mistake, however, to think that large sampling errors matter any less than large non-sampling errors. To a data user, large errors are equally serious regardless of their source.

It is certainly not accurate to suggest that my papers do not discuss the role of bias and its consequences: that is what my papers are all about. My treatment of sampling error, however, is very brief but very pertinent:

> There are several types of measurement error. Although the point being made here is that the large amount of error in the adjustments is consistent with the thesis that large amounts of *non-sampling* error are inevitable, it should be noted that *sampling* error is also a very serious problem for the undercount adjustments. Actually, there

and Howard Hogan, U.S. Bureau of the Census, "Statistical Methodologies for Census 2000: Decisions, Issues, and Preliminary Results," presented at the American Statistical Association Joint Statistical Meetings, Section on Social Statistics, August 13, 1998.

is more than enough error to go around: these adjustments can reflect a very large amount of sampling error as well as a very large amount of non-sampling error. For purposes of data quality, both types of error are very problematic.

The role of sampling error is discussed in more detail in my letter to Representative Maloney dated June 19, 1998, in response to the twenty-five questions that she posed subsequent to my testimony to the Subcommittee on the Census. The limitations of sampling error as an explanation for the shortcomings of the undercount adjustments are discussed in response to Question 16, and the limited impact of a larger sample size on total error and sampling error is discussed in response to Questions 17 and 20.[2]

In summary, the bureau's response does not address my arguments directly, and the points that it does raise do not weaken my arguments.

Some Implications of Faulty Adjustments. *Inaccurate adjustments would destroy the reliability of census data at the state and local level.*

(a) *Errors would sometimes be large.*

(b) *Errors for a given segment of the population can be expected to differ from one census to another, which would invalidate comparisons of census data over time.*

(c) *These errors would have a serious impact on policy decisions and on our understanding of trends in our communities.*

---

2. The key point to be emphasized here is that the bureau has documented huge biases and other non-sampling errors as well as huge sampling errors. It is an obvious fallacy to presume that the seriousness of non-sampling error is mitigated in any way by the seriousness of sampling error. To say "We do not need to look any further than sampling error to explain the problems with the adjustments" is to ignore the fact that—regardless of whether one chooses to look at them—huge levels of non-sampling error have also been documented. Ignoring those errors will not make them go away.

(d) *The presence of significant unpredictable errors would make all census comparisons unreliable. When the census suggested a change in population trends, data users would not know how much of the change represented actual demographic trends and how much represented spurious differences in the undercount adjustments.*

Status: Subpoint (a) and subpoint (c) are addressed but not refuted. The other points are not addressed.

The bureau's memorandum makes the following two arguments:

1. Subpoint (a) is addressed by stating:

This example (that is, the spurious differential undercounts for children) is misleading. The undercounts of 10, 20, and 30 percent are rare exceptions, and did not occur for major segments of the population. In fact, in subsequent analyses, we find that only 2 poststrata in the final set of 357 PES poststrata were over 20 percent, 10 were from 15 to 20 percent, and 17 were 10 to 15 percent. In short, 328 of the 357 poststrata were less than 10 percent—not grounds for devastating impacts.

This statement raises several issues and questions.

- The bureau argues that large adjustments are "rare exceptions," but then points out that nearly 8 percent of the 357 final "collapsed" adjustments were over ten percentage points—certainly opportunity enough for a substantial number of serious errors to occur.
- Large adjustments were even more frequent for the initial non-smoothed factors, which are the ones most pertinent to the analysis in my paper and most pertinent to the methodology proposed for Census 2000: 218 (16 percent) of the 1,392 non-smoothed adjustment factors ex-

ceeded ten percentage points, ranging from a downward adjustment of 36 percent to an upward adjustment of 51 percent.

• What does the Census Bureau consider to be a "minor" segment of the population for which large errors would be acceptable? As one looks at the specifications for the 357 collapsed poststrata (or, more pertinently, the specifications for the eighteen pairs of poststrata for which undercount rates are listed in figure 3 of my paper), none of them appears to be unimportant or insignificant. The census is often relied upon for data on small segments of the population. If the community or population group on which a data user must focus is one of the ones affected by large errors, it would be of little comfort to know that most of the errors elsewhere are smaller.

• How "large" would an error have to be to be serious? Although the differential undercounts that my paper demonstrates to be spurious all exceed ten percentage points, it should be noted that even much smaller errors can be serious. Differences of a few percentage points or a few tenths of a percentage point can have significant implications for policy decisions, for resource distribution, and for understanding demographic trends in our communities.

• The impact of any errors is compounded by the fact that data users would not know which areas and population groups have serious errors and which do not. The uncertainty resulting from large errors hidden throughout the data from the next census—regardless of whether they are hidden thickly or sparsely—would have a "devastating impact" by itself.

• Finally, it should be noted that the spurious undercounts identified in my paper are accurately described and they are pertinent to the conclusions that are drawn from them. They therefore would not have been "misleading" even if the comments in the bureau's memorandum were valid.

125

2. With regard to the hypothetical examples used to illustrate subpoint (c), the bureau states:

> Given what we know about the small sample sizes and high variances of the estimates for children under ten, Mr. Darga's use of age data to speculate about demographic trends of Asians or black homeowners is very misleading and inappropriate.

I have several responses to this observation:

• I will readily grant that the adjustments for children under ten reflect very high levels of sampling error (as well as very high levels of non-sampling error). If the statement quoted above is intended to imply that the estimates for different age groups are less beset by these problems, then some evidence to that effect should be provided.

• The argument that these illustrations are misleading and inappropriate seems to be based on the observation that the sampling error for a very small group (for example, persons *under the age of ten* within a particular segment of the population) would tend to be higher than the sampling error for a somewhat larger group (for example, persons *of all ages* within that segment of the population). If the variability of the adjustment factors from one census to another were solely due to statistically "well-behaved" sampling error, this criticism of the illustrations would have merit. However, several additional sources of variability must be considered:

• Methodologies used in the coverage survey can change significantly from one census to the next. For example, changes planned between 1990 and 2000 include computing adjustment factors for individual states instead of for multi-state regions, a shorter period of time in which to conduct interviews, and a different choice of weeks for interviews.

• A given state might have a spell of hot or rainy weather during one PES but not during the next. This can significantly affect several factors that influence the adjustments, including the rate of successful interviews, the percentage of homeless people who are found in households, and the percent of interviews fabricated by enumerators.

• The undercount rates for a given area might be strongly affected by a few aberrant blocks for one census but not for another. An extreme example of the impact of aberrant blocks is the two block clusters (out of a total of 5,290) that by themselves would have accounted for about 15 percent of the net national undercount in 1990 due to geocoding errors if they had not been identified and corrected. Of course, block clusters *cannot* be divided neatly into two groups: those for which errors are blatantly obvious and those for which the measure of undercount is practically perfect. Block clusters can be aberrant for many reasons. There can be a severe or modest number of geocoding errors, a new housing development, a large number of seasonal dwellings, a university with exams during the period in which census interviews are conducted, a retirement community or another special population group, a bad census enumerator, a bad PES enumerator. . . . The list of examples is endless. As demonstrated by the example above, a few aberrant blocks can cause variations even greater than those in the illustrations in question.

• Finally, it should be noted that the illustrations in question do not really "speculate about demographic trends of Asians or black homeowners." Rather, they are used to illustrate how variations in error levels from one census to the next would have serious implications. Regardless of whether one likes the hypothetical examples that are used to make this point, the point itself still remains.

Relevance to Census 2000. *The problems with the 1990 adjustments can be expected to recur in Census 2000 if the proposed* *methodology is used. They are not due to minor correctable flaws in methodology or implementation, but rather to the impossibility of measuring undercount through the proposed coverage survey.*

Status: Discussed but not refuted.

Most of the arguments in my papers involve problems that are either inherent in the effort to measure undercount with a post-enumeration survey, or else so intractable that they cannot be corrected.

The bureau addresses this argument by asserting:

> We do not share Mr. Darga's view that measuring the undercount with a coverage survey is impossible, though we do concede it is a challenging task. Furthermore, Mr. Darga fails to acknowledge years of research and development since the 1990 Census. The statement deliberately ignores the progress that has been made in our understanding of ways to improve data collection and data processing. Technological innovations to facilitate quality control and improve coverage have been adopted for implementation in the 2000 Census. Throughout the decade, we have continued to enhance our knowledge about the causes of undercount and census coverage errors in general. Of course, the lessons learned and the progress made are of little relevance to Mr. Darga's position, but that does not undo the reality of their existence.

Although I am aware of several innovations planned for the next census and the next post-enumeration survey, I am not aware of any that would enable the next post-enumeration survey to succeed where the previous one failed. If there are such innovations, I invite the bureau to show specifically how they negate each of the arguments in my papers. Until that is done, I must agree that "the lessons learned and the progress made are of little relevance to Mr. Darga's position."

Matching Error. *The key to measuring undercount with a coverage survey is to match each person's survey record with the corresponding census record. However, when the same records were matched by different teams of trained personnel using the same definitions and guidelines, the disagreement rate was very high relative to the size of the net undercount that the 1990 Post-Enumeration Survey was trying to measure. Implications of this finding include:*

(a) *The number of difficult cases for which match status is not obvious is very large, greatly exceeding the estimated level of net undercount. This demonstrates the impossibility of measuring undercount accurately through a coverage survey even apart from any other considerations.*

(b) *The high level of disagreement suggests that many of the judgments reached by the final team of matchers are likely to be wrong.*

(c) *The level of subjectivity demonstrated by the high rate of disagreement makes the adjustments vulnerable to bias through expectations and other impertinent factors.*

(d) *The high level of disagreement between matchers causes the results for a given set of records to be different each time the match is performed.*

Status: Not addressed.

Fabrication of Data. *Fabrication of data by interviewers is another problem that is sufficient by itself to invalidate the adjustments for undercount derived from a post-enumeration survey.*

(a) *The level of fabrication in typical Census Bureau surveys is very substantial relative to the level of net undercount that the post-enumeration survey attempts to measure.*

(b) *Fabrication in either the census or the PES can cause very serious errors in the undercount adjustments.*

(c) *Taken together, the three studies of fabrication in the 1990 PES suggest that its level of fabrication may have been close to the level found in other Census Bureau surveys.*

(d) *Apparent levels of fabrication varied substantially among*

regions. The regions that appeared to have the highest levels of fabrication were regions with high adjustments for undercount, and they also had very hot or rainy weather during the period in which PES interviews were conducted.

Status: Not addressed.

Ambiguous "Usual" Place of Residence. *The number of people with an ambiguous "usual" place of residence poses serious problems for undercount adjustments derived from a coverage survey.*

(a) *The number of people with an ambiguous "usual" place of residence is very substantial relative to the level of net undercount.*

(b) *The adjustments derived from the coverage survey can have a significant impact on the regional population distribution by replacing the traditional concept of "usual" address, which is defined largely by the respondent, with a set of assignment rules developed for the coverage survey.*

(c) *Neighborhoods vary greatly in their proportion of people with an indistinct "usual" place of residence. The adjustments for a class of cities in an entire state or region can be determined largely by whether or not the sample includes a few blocks that are outliers in this respect.*

Status: Not addressed.

Geocoding Errors. *Geocoding errors pose very serious problems for undercount adjustments derived from a coverage survey.*

(a) *Geocoding errors can cause errors in classifying people as missed by the census, correctly enumerated, or erroneously enumerated. These errors can cause bias in the undercount adjustments, since they do not necessarily cancel one another out.*

(b) *The size of the net undercount is very sensitive to the size of the search area for records with inaccurate geographic codes. This illustrates the sensitivity of the undercount adjustments*

> *to minor variations in the procedure for conducting and analyzing the coverage survey.*
>
> *(c) Geocoding errors in only two block clusters (out of a total of 5,290) caused them to contribute nearly a million people to a preliminary calculation of net undercount. This illustrates the extreme sensitivity of the undercount adjustments to small errors, their sensitivity to a few outlier blocks, and the importance of minor variations in methodology such as criteria and methods for correcting errors that are discovered.*

Status: Not addressed.

Unreliable Interviews. *Unreliable interviews pose a very serious problem for undercount adjustments derived from a coverage survey. The percent of records that changed match status due to different information in re-interviews conducted for evaluation purposes was very large relative to the level of net undercount.*

Status: Not addressed.

Unresolvable Cases. *The number of cases in the 1990 Post-Enumeration Survey that were unresolved even after repeated interview attempts was very substantial relative to the level of net undercount. The uncertainty resulting from such a large number of unresolved cases is a fatal flaw in the undercount measurements.*

Status: Not addressed.

Combined Impact of Errors. *A very substantial proportion of the apparent net undercount identified through the 1990 coverage survey was actually caused by bias due to various errors that were identified and documented in the Census Bureau's evaluation reports. In other words, it turned out that many of the people identified as "missed" by the census actually had not been missed at all.*

Status: Discussed but not refuted.

The bureau responded to this argument by stating:

131

It was the finding that at the U.S. level, *when correlation bias is taken into account,* about 22 percent of the revised estimate of undercount (1.6 percent) was bias and not measured undercount. This is substantially less than the figure claimed by Mr. Darga. Even if the effect of correlation bias is ignored, our estimate of bias is well below the 70 percent referenced by Mr. Darga. It also should be noted that while Mr. Darga spends considerable time discussing non-sampling errors via short illustrations, no mention is made of what we actually know about the effects of these errors [emphasis added].

The disagreement on this point between my paper and the bureau's memorandum is much smaller than it may seem at first: I make no objection to the figures which the bureau cites, except to note that they are not as pertinent to my arguments as the figures from the same studies that are cited in my papers.

My observations with respect to the bureau's comments are as follows:

• Attributing 22 percent of the national undercount adjustments to bias should provide very scant comfort to proponents of adjustment. Even if the bias problem were no worse than that, a 22 percent bias would be sufficient to invalidate the adjustments.

• An overall national estimate of bias—whether the 22 percent figure cited by the bureau or the more pertinent figures described below—reflects some areas and some segments of the population that have higher levels of bias and others that have lower bias or even bias in the opposite direction. Admitting an overall bias of 22 percent therefore amounts to an admission that some parts of the country have adjustment factors that are in error by more than 22 percent.

• The 22 percent figure cited by the bureau reflects the amount of bias that remains *after incorporating the effects of correlation bias.* This is perfectly consistent with the central thesis of my papers, that is, that a post-enumeration survey cannot provide a reliable basis for adjusting the census for undercount because (a) a post-enumeration survey misses many of the same people that are missed by the census ("correlation bias"), and (b) many of the people it identifies as "missed" by the census really have not been missed at all. Based on the Census Bureau's "demographic analysis" findings, I have suggested that these two errors largely cancel one another out with respect to the overall national measure of undercount. The bureau here suggests that the two errors do not come quite so close to canceling one another out: they contend that the undercount estimates still have a 22 percent upward bias even after incorporating the effects of correlation bias. Although the inconsistency between this figure and the findings of demographic analysis leads me to be somewhat skeptical of it, I am willing to accept it at face value for purposes of this discussion since, as explained below, it is irrelevant to the figures in my paper that the bureau is attempting to challenge.

• The 70 percent figure that the bureau attempts to challenge is used in my paper to make the argument that a large number of people are falsely identified as "missed" by the census, and that they are *subsequently* offset by correlation bias. Obviously, the pertinent figure to use for such a purpose would *not* already subtract the effects of correlation bias.

• There are at least two reasons why the bureau's estimate of bias is below the 70 percent figure cited in my paper even when they do not subtract the effects of correlation bias. The first reason would be evident from a more careful reading of my paper:

> The analysis in the Census Bureau's P-16 report indicates that the corrections for measurement errors in the 1990 PES would have decreased the

undercount estimate from 2.1 percent to 1.4 percent [that is, about 33 percent]. . . . A later analysis by the same author incorporated additional corrections related to a major computer processing error discovered by the Census Bureau in late 1991, the re-matching of records in some suspect blocks, and the inclusion of very late census data that had not been available when the initial PES estimates were developed. This analysis suggested that corrections for identified measurement errors would have reduced the undercount estimate from 2.1 percent to 0.9 percent [that is, about 57 percent]. . . . An analysis by Dr. Leo Breiman, which built on the Census Bureau analyses cited above, incorporated additional sources of error to arrive at an adjusted undercount estimate of only 0.6 percent [that is, about 70 percent lower than the 2.1 percent figure].

Thus, one of the reasons why the bureau's figures are different from mine is that they do not take into account all of the factors that were included in Dr. Breiman's analysis. While it is certainly true that 33 percent and 57 percent are lower than 70 percent, it is hardly noteworthy. Another reason for the discrepancy is not quite so obvious: my figures are intended to reflect all of the identified errors in the adjustments that had been proposed for the 1990 Census counts, but the figures cited in the bureau's Memorandum for the Record reflect only errors that the bureau did not subsequently correct. The errors that the bureau chose to correct are just as pertinent to my arguments as the errors that the bureau identified but did not correct.

- I am puzzled by the statement that:

    While Mr. Darga spends considerable time discussing non-sampling errors via short illustrations, no mention is made of what we actually know about the effects of these errors.

I certainly try to mention the things that *I* know about the effect of those errors. I invite the bureau to share its additional insights regarding the effects of these errors, and to indicate how they amplify or refute each of the arguments in my papers.

Counterarguments Raised by the Census Bureau

The Census Bureau's Memorandum for the Record raises several counterarguments that are not associated with any of the individual arguments raised in my paper:

Focus on Underlying Data Instead of Subsequent Calculations. *The bureau's memorandum states:*

> *Mr. Darga is so determined to focus on the coverage survey itself that he fails to acknowledge the strengths of the DSE [Dual-System Estimation] methodology that makes use of the data. The focus is strictly on data collection and the subsequent matching operation associated with the PES. No attempt is made to fully describe all the steps involved in the PES, or to explain the DSE methodology and the statistical model of capture-recapture. Had Mr. Darga focused on the DSE methodology rather than the coverage measurement survey itself, he would probably not have stated "that based on what was provided by the Census Bureau in 1990, one could be tempted to draw the conclusion that a coverage survey can provide an incredibly accurate measure of census undercount. . . ." The PES does not directly provide the undercount rate. It provides the data to be used for developing adjustment factors based on the DSE methodology.*

I have several observations with respect to this counterargument:

• Addressing the last point first, it is true that, strictly speaking, the Post-Enumeration Survey produces only raw

data. The subsequent analysis of that data involves matching survey records with census records and using the results of that matching process in a formula to produce
the actual undercount adjustments. Like other writings on
this subject, my papers sometimes use the terms "coverage
survey" or "PES" to encompass the survey itself, the subsequent analysis, and the results of that analysis. See, for
example, the statement in the bureau's Memorandum for
the Record:

> We would go so far as to argue that the agree-
> ment between the 1990 PES and demographic
> analysis on the undercount rate is more than a
> happy coincidence

I would also add that the phrases that are presented as a
quotation from my paper appear to be merely a para-
phrase by a Census Bureau analyst. The sentence that actually appears in my paper is:

> Thus, one is tempted to conclude that data from
> a coverage survey can provide an incredibly accu-
> rate measure of census undercount.

• Turning to the more substantial point raised in the
bureau's argument, I readily agree that my papers focus
on the coverage survey and on the data developed for use
in the adjustment formula rather than on the adjustment
formula itself. In my first statistics course as an undergrad-
uate, I was taught that the Fundamental Law of Statistics is
"Garbage in, garbage out." If the Dual System Estimation
methodology has the ability to produce correct and reliable adjustments by treating survey findings as accurate
when they are in fact dominated by measurement errors,
I invite the bureau to explain exactly how that is accomplished. Until that is done, I will assume that the Fundamental Law of Statistics is still in effect.

• It is also true that my papers do not use the term
"capture-recapture methodology." Although I have tried

to avoid technical terminology and theoretical discussions as much as possible in my papers, it is nonetheless fruitful to review the capture-recapture model and the assumptions upon which it relies.

The capture-recapture model is most widely used in wildlife biology. A common illustration is that, if you catch and mark a certain number of fish on one day, you can estimate the total number of fish in the lake by catching some fish on another day, and then assuming that the proportion of fish with marks tells you the proportion of the total fish population that was caught on the first day. For example, if 50 percent of the fish that you catch on the second day have marks, you assume that you had marked 50 percent of the fish in the lake on the first day.

As any fisherman can probably guess, this method does not always produce accurate results. According to George Seber's *Estimation of Animal Abundance and Related Parameters*,[3] this sort of capture-recapture model can produce suitable results when certain assumptions are met, such as:

(a) The population is closed so that N is constant. (This assumption is obviously violated in the attempt to measure undercount with a coverage survey. A substantial number of people are born, die, or move from one place to another between the census and the survey. It is very difficult to compensate for this problem, and it is one of the serious sources of error discussed in chapters 2 and 3.)

(b) All animals have the same probability of being caught in the first sample. (In the context of measuring undercount in the U.S. Census, this assumption translates into a premise that all people within a poststratum—that is, within a designated component

---

3. George Seber, *Estimation of Animal Abundance and Related Parameters* (New York: 1982).

of the population—have the same probability of being counted in the census. As discussed above, however, some people purposely avoid being counted by the census, and others are not counted because of various other factors that make them difficult to count. Thus, this assumption is also violated.)

(c) Marking does not affect the catchability of an animal. (In the context of measuring undercount in the U.S. Census, this translates into a premise that people counted by the census are just as likely to be counted in the coverage survey as people in the same poststratum who are missed by the census. Obviously, when people are missed because they want to be missed or because they are particularly difficult to count, this assumption is not met.)

(d) Animals do not lose their marks in the time between the two samples, and all marks are reported on recovery in the second sample. (In the context of measuring undercount in the U.S. Census, this assumption translates into a premise that all of the people in the sample who were counted by the census are successfully matched with their census records. One reason for the failure of the matching process is that the marking techniques used by wildlife biologists are not suitable for use by census enumerators. Thus, as discussed at length in my papers, people counted by the census can be falsely classified as having been missed.)

Thus, one way of summarizing many of the arguments in my papers is to say that the Census Bureau's methodology for developing undercount adjustments violates the fundamental assumptions upon which the underlying capture-recapture model is based.

Sufficiency of PES Data. *The bureau's memorandum states:*

> *The record should also reflect that the PES data were deemed of sufficient high quality to do so [sic] on the*

basis of evaluation criteria that were accepted and agreed upon prior to the 1990 census. Given the facts, Mr. Darga has no valid basis to conclude that adjustments based on the PES in 1990 "would have had a devastating impact on the usefulness and accuracy of census data at the state and local level."

This seems to say that the 1990 undercount adjustments were good enough to be used for the 1990 Census. This overlooks the fact that the secretary of commerce decided not to apply the 1990 adjustments to the census, and the director of the Census Bureau decided not to apply them to the intercensal estimates. These decisions were based on sound arguments, as demonstrated by the explanations that accompanied them.[4]

The sentence that begins "Given the facts . . ." is difficult to reply to, since no facts appear either in this paragraph or in the remainder of the bureau's memorandum that support the subsequent statement. If the bureau is aware of such facts, they should be presented along with an explanation of how they negate the arguments above.

Arguments Presented Are Not New. *The bureau's memorandum states:*

> *The arguments and viewpoints presented by Mr. Darga are not new to the adjustment debate and have entered into many adjustment deliberations. . . . Powerful arguments about coverage measurement have been made in support of adjustment of the decennial census as well as against adjustment.*

If the bureau's Memorandum for the Record is any indication, the fact that these arguments are not new should not at all suggest that they have been refuted.

I agree that the evidence about the undercount ad-

---

4. See *Federal Register,* July 22, 1991, pp. 33582–33642, and *Federal Register,* January 4, 1993, pp. 69–78.

justments presents a paradox. On the one hand, there is very strong evidence to show that the undercount adjustments are based on a variety of very serious errors. And yet, on the other hand, there are some respects in which the undercount adjustments look like one would expect valid adjustments to look. A paradox should *not*, however, be seen as an opportunity to simply choose which evidence one wishes to accept and which evidence one wishes to ignore. A paradox demands an explanation. Either the contradictory evidence must be refuted, or else a new understanding must be reached through which the apparent contradiction can be resolved. Throughout my papers, I have therefore attempted to explain how the apparent strengths of the adjustments can be explained in the context of their weaknesses.

One of the most powerful arguments in favor of the adjustments has been the "remarkable" closeness of the overall net national undercount suggested by the 1990 PES to the overall net national undercount suggested by demographic analysis. This apparent strength of the adjustments, however, can be explained very well in the context of their weaknesses:

- My papers show this finding to result from missing a lot of the same people who were missed by the census, and then identifying a similar number of people as having been missed when they actually were not missed at all.
- The closeness of the two results also reflects the influence of expectations about undercount on the adjustment factors.

Another powerful argument in favor of the adjustment factors is the (very rough) similarity between the groups that tend to have high adjustment factors and the groups that would be expected to have high undercounts. This apparent strength of the adjustments can also be explained in the context of their weaknesses:

140

- It reflects a substantial overlap between the groups that are hard to count and the groups for which it is difficult to match survey records with census records.

- It reflects the fact that fabrication of records, which tends to cause a low match rate and a high apparent level of undercount, tends to be more frequent in neighborhoods that interviewers perceive as dangerous.

- It reflects the role of expectations in determining whether an uncertain survey case will be classified as "matched" or "not matched" with the census.

Perhaps the greatest paradox involves the enormous error rates identified in the Census Bureau's evaluations of the 1990 Post-Enumeration Survey: how can such high levels of error be consistent with the high levels of skill and care with which the PES was obviously conducted? Perhaps the Census Bureau's readiness to reject the evidence against the PES without refuting it rests upon a failure to resolve this paradox. To those familiar with the skill, credentials, and conscientiousness of the team that designed and implemented the PES, the error levels identified by the Census Bureau's evaluations must seem unbelievable. Nevertheless, there is a resolution for this paradox as well. Given the extreme sensitivity of a coverage survey to very small mistakes and the many serious sources of mistakes, it is inevitable for the adjustments to be dominated by errors in measuring undercount. It is not the documented failure of the adjustment methodology that is unbelievable, but rather the blithe assumption that skill and hard work can overcome the fatal flaws inherent in the bureau's methodology.

Thus, the arguments presented here not only make a strong case against the proposed methodology, but they also show how its apparent strengths are consistent with its documented weaknesses. In order to prevail in the current debate, the Census Bureau must either refute the sixteen arguments listed above, or else show in a similar manner that the unrefuted arguments can somehow be made consistent with the thesis that we can count on the undercount adjustments to be highly accurate. I believe that this task will prove to be as impossible as deriving accurate undercount adjustments from a coverage survey.

About the Author

KENNETH DARGA has been senior demographer at the Michigan Department of Management and Budget since 1991. He has served as a member of the steering committee of the Federal-State Cooperative Program for Population Estimates, and he is a member of a Census Bureau work group on post-2000 population estimation methodology. He holds a B.A. from Boston College and Master's degrees from the University of Michigan in both public policy and economic demography.

A NOTE ON THE BOOK

This book was edited by Cheryl Weissman
of the publications staff
of the American Enterprise Institute.
The figures were drawn by Hördur Karlsson.
The text was set in New Baskerville.
Coghill Composition Company, of
Richmond, Virginia, set the type,
and Edward Brothers, Incorporated, of
Lillington, North Carolina,
printed and bound the book
using permanent acid-free paper.

The AEI Press is the publisher for the American Enterprise Institute for Public Policy Research, 1150 Seventeenth Street, N.W., Washington, D.C. 20036; *Christopher C. DeMuth,* publisher; *Ann Petty,* editor; *Leigh Tripoli,* editor; *Cheryl Weissman,* editor; *Alice Anne English,* managing editor; *Susanna Huang,* editorial production assistant.